COVID Dispatches

*Pondering a Pandemic
and a Most Unusual Year*

Steve Elderbrock

Parson's Porch Books

COVID Dispatches: Pondering a Pandemic and a Most Unusual Year

ISBN: Softcover 978-1-951472-91-7

Copyright © 2021 by Steve Elderbrock

All rights reserved. No part of this book may be reproduced or transmitted in any form or by any means, electronic or mechanical, including photocopying, recording, or by any information storage and retrieval system, without permission in writing from the publisher.

COVID Dispatches

Preface

March 1, 2021

On Saturday, March 14, 2020, with COVID-19 beginning to rage in this country, the Session of First Presbyterian Church and I decided we should heed the warnings about in-person activities and cancel Sunday worship for the next day.

Little did any of us realize we would remain closed for in-person worship for next 11 months and likely for at least the next couple months ahead, even as people begin to receive the COVID vaccine. We felt we should always put people's health and safety before any other consideration.

That Saturday, I sent out an email to our church family informing them about our decision. The following day, unable to preach my prepared sermon in worship, I decided to email my notes and reflections to the church family instead.

Even though we began offering a virtual online Sunday worship service a couple weeks later, I continued to send out my daily email reflection and I have continued that practice every day since (except for vacation time) up until the present moment. That's well over 300 such daily reflections, and in that time I have ranged over topics related to the feast days of saints, historic events of that particular day in history, the writings of Thomas Merton (*for many months I shared quotes from Merton on what I called "Merton Mondays"*), poetry (*as I ran out of quotes from Thomas Merton, Merton Mondays became "Poetry Mondays"*) and even some personal reflections on my life. The lectionary I use which provides the spark for these reflections is based on the Book of Common Worship and reflects the readings authorized by the Church of England for daily and weekly services.

In this book you will find thirty selected daily reflections, most of them relating to the pandemic and our response to it as followers of Christ. Although these are specific reflections for a specific time, I certainly hope they have wider application and speak to the larger picture of how we can do our best to live as followers of Christ, pandemic or no pandemic.

I also hope and pray that you, the reader, will find inspiration in these reflections, wherever you are along your journey of faith, as well.

Thank you for reading, stay well, and may peace be with you!

Sunday, March 15, 2020

Friends,

Since we were not able to physically gather this morning for worship, I wanted to pass along the Scripture reading we would have read and a brief summary of some of the reflections I was intending to share in my sermon today.

Today's reading is **John 4:5-42**, the story of Jesus encountering a Samaritan woman at Jacob's well.

This is a fascinating passage, partly because it is one of the longest conversations recorded in the New Testament, certainly one of the longest recorded with Jesus. In it, Jesus confronts and overturns many social conventions, including the fact that Jews didn't usually associate with Samaritans, and especially Jewish men with Samaritan women. Yet Jesus engages in a very deep, spiritual conversation with this unnamed woman, and treats her as an equal. He patiently answers her questions and in essence guides her as her faith and understanding grow before our eyes. He knows her and sees her as a fellow child of God. He doesn't rebuke her when she misunderstands what he is saying nor does he judge her or condemn her when she reveals that she has had five husbands *(we don't know why she has had five husbands — it could be a situation akin to the question the Sadducees pose to Jesus in Luke 20:27-33 about a woman whose husband dies and each brother marries her and then dies so the next one steps in — we just don't know the details of the Samaritan woman's life...although Jesus clearly does).*

I also find it fascinating that at the end of this passage, this unnamed Samaritan woman has grown from being a questioner to an evangelist – she goes into her town and begins to spread the good news about Jesus, and people respond. *(This is yet another passage, like the Easter story, which clearly shows a woman preaching and sharing the good news – just a reminder that Jesus allowed, even encouraged, woman to be preachers and teachers, despite what usually male-dominated denominations have sometimes decided in the centuries since).*

In this passage, Jesus talks about "living water" and "food" that his disciples know nothing about, clearly references to spiritual nourishment from God. I would remind you in these strange times with COVID-19 and uncertainty and anxiety that Jesus still offers us this spiritual nourishment, this living water and food for the soul. I would encourage you to find ways in these next days and weeks to nourish your soul through prayer, meditation, reading, study, and simply resting in the security of God's presence.

The last comment I wanted to share *(there is a lot more that could be said about this rich passage, and more that I was hoping to say in today's sermon, but I will keep these reflections brief)* is about what Jesus says about worship. The Samaritans, despite a shared heritage with the Jews, worshipped God on Mount Gerizim in Samaria, rather than travelling to Jerusalem to the Temple. When the Samaritan woman asks Jesus about this, he says: **"Believe me, woman, the time is coming when you and your people will worship the Father neither on this mountain nor in Jerusalem. You and your people worship what you don't know; we worship what we know because salvation is from the Jews. But the time is coming—and** *is here!—when true worshippers will worship in spirit and truth. The Father looks for those who worship him this way. God is spirit, and it is necessary to worship God in spirit and truth."* (John 4:21-24)

In other words, the time is coming (and is here) when WHERE you worship, the PLACE, does not truly matter. What matters to God is that we worship honestly and authentically, in "spirit and in truth." We are in a moment when we are not able to worship together in person, in a specific place – a church building and sanctuary that we love – BUT we can still worship, and worship together, across physical space. For we are still one body, the body of Christ, even when separate. The lack of physical contact does not and should not lessen our spiritual journey together – in fact, it might even enhance it, as we figure out what it means to be in community while physically distance. I would invite you to reflect and pray upon this idea this week. And know that we are still bound together by spirit and truth and faith and prayers and God.

Peace be with each and every one of you, until we gather again.

Pastor Steve

Sunday, March 22, 2020

Friends,

For the second Sunday we are unable to be together, physically, for worship. But I wanted to share some reflections on the readings I had intended to be preaching on today in my planning before the Coronavirus hit.

The main reading I had intended to focus on is **John chapter 9** – the story of Jesus healing a man blind from birth, and the reaction of the man, the Pharisees, the crowds, and everyone to this miraculous event, performed (*gasp!*) on the Sabbath.

But my focus has shifted in the past 2 weeks since I began thinking about today's sermon. Now what really jumps out at me in this story is something Jesus says at the very beginning of this passage. Jesus and his disciples see this man, blind since birth, and the disciples ask Jesus whose sin caused this man to be blind – his own or his parents *(because, clearly, someone has to be at fault, right?)* Jesus replies: **"Neither this man nor his parents sinned; he was born blind so that God's works might be revealed in him. We must work the works of him who sent me while it is day; night is coming when no one can work."**

So given all that has happened in the past couple weeks, two things now jump out at me here:

1) We humans like to find someone to blame for tragic events, and we see this with the Coronavirus as well. Sure, it started in

China, and sure, our federal government's response has been disjointed and slow, but perhaps no one is to blame for all this, really...or perhaps we should focus less on assigning blame and more on trying to contain the virus and respond to those in need *(more on that in a minute)*. What is really important to focus on is how God is at work even in such awful and disruptive events. I am hopeful that good can and will come out of all this – a renewed appreciation, perhaps, for community and social organizations and the pleasures of boring, normal everyday life. Perhaps we will emerge better and stronger and more compassionate as individuals, if not as a society. As Fred Rogers so famously once said, in situations like this, let's look for the helpers and keep our eyes on them.

2) Jesus says we must work now because a time is coming when we will not be able to work. Well, folks, some people are literally in that moment right now – unable to work. People are being told to stay home, to self-quarantine; businesses, especially small businesses, are closing or reducing their staff and their hours. We find ourselves, in a sense *(a very literal sense)* in that "night" that Jesus talked about. And the question remains – how will we respond? How does God want us to respond? As individuals, as a community of faith, and as a nation and a global community? I must admit, until this week I had never thought about those words of Jesus in quite this way...and I continue to ponder them and how they might relate to this moment we find ourselves in.

Psalm 23 also appears in the lectionary of readings for this 4th Sunday of Lent. And what better time to read and reconsider this familiar, comforting Psalm?

"The Lord is my shepherd; I shall not want." Hmmm, in a moment in time when people are hoarding toilet paper and bread and other such things *(the shelves at Ingles this morning were pretty bare, especially those aisles)* this simple sentence speaks volumes. We have the Lord as our shepherd, watching over us, guarding and guiding us – what more do we really need or want? And our Lord supplies our deepest needs – even deeper than toilet paper and bread *(remember, one does not live by bread alone, but by every word that comes from God, as Jesus reminded the devil in the wilderness)*. This is a good time to count our blessings and focus on all that we DO have, too. How blessed we are, even in the midst of this Coronavirus situation.

"He maketh me to lie down in green pastures: he leadeth me beside the still waters. He restoreth my soul" Every time I read these words I can almost feel my heart beat slowing and my body relaxing. God promises us rest and peace and restoration of our souls, even *(especially)* in uncertain and anxious times such as these. I'd encourage you to get outside to enjoy the goodness of God's creation, even if in your own backyard. Find some version of green pastures and still waters to help restore your soul, and your courage, with God's help.

"Yea, though I walk through the valley of the shadow of death, I will fear no evil: for thou art with me" Friends, I'd say we are in a moment when lots of individuals, and our entire world, are walking through the valley of the shadow of death. We don't know for sure how many people have this potentially deadly virus yet, and even getting within 6 feet of another human being might bring this virus your way. These are scary times, and they certainly qualify as being "in the valley of the shadow of death." But we need fear no evil, we need not be afraid…because our God is with us, our good shepherd is with us. This doesn't necessarily offer us physical protection from the virus, but it does offer us a sure vaccine against fear and anxiety and panic. God is with you, even if you are all alone, self-quarantined in your house. Because your house is God's house, too…

"Surely goodness and mercy shall follow me all the days of my life: and I will dwell in the house of the Lord for ever." Your house is God's house, as much as our church sanctuary is God's house, as much as the Temple there in Jerusalem in the time of Jesus was God's house. Even when we can't gather for worship together in God's house, we can gather spiritually through prayer and worship in our own houses, knowing God is with us, and we are there in spirit together. And we can be certain that God's goodness and God's mercy are also with us (and ours to share with others, too).

I invite you to rest in and with this wonderful Psalm today, and ponder what else God may be saying to you through it.

I miss seeing you all, but will keep doing my best to stay in touch via phone and email and social media…

May the peace of Christ be with each and every one of you, until we are able to gather again,

Pastor Steve

Thursday, March 26, 2020

Friends,

These verses from the Book of Hebrews jumped off the page at me this morning:

**"Let us hold unswervingly to the hope we profess,
for he who promised is faithful.
And let us consider how we may spur one another on toward love and good deeds,
not giving up meeting together, as some are in the habit of doing,
but encouraging one another—and all the more as you see the Day approaching."**
Hebrews 10:23-25

First of all, the irony of "not giving up meeting together" actually made me chuckle. I'm sure the writer of Hebrews was not considering public health concerns during a global pandemic in any way when writing those words. What he was talking about was people, even in those days, developing the "habit" of not meeting together, devaluing the necessity and meaning of community when it comes to following Christ. Obviously the Session and I have cancelled worship through April 1 for all the right reasons, but I must admit I am concerned that this may get some of us in the habit of not meeting. I hope not. I hope instead that not being able to gather for worship and prayer and fellowship will have the opposite effect of reminding us all how much we miss being together, and that the first Sunday we are able to worship together again the sanctuary will be packed full.

I love the reminder in this passage about why we can hold onto hope, even when things might look dark or hopeless. We can keep hoping because God, the one "who promised" is faithful. Our hope is based on faith and trust in God who, up until now, has never let us down. God doesn't always provide in exactly the way we might like or as quickly as we want, but God is faithful and trustworthy and we can keep hoping – and praying.

I also love what the writer invites us to do while we continue to hope and trust in God: *"let us consider how we might spur one another on toward love and good deeds...encouraging one another"*. This seems all the more important in these times we are living in. Let's keep finding ways to support each other, encourage each other, and spur each other on to doing good in whatever ways we can, even if we are stuck at home. We can still pray. We can still phone people that might be feeling lonely and anxious. We can still send cards and letters and emails to check in with people and to remind them that we are thinking of them and praying for them. We can donate supplies and financial resources to charities that support those on the front lines of this healthcare crisis. There are lots of creative ways we can find to keep in touch and support each other and encourage each other and do good, even from the confines of our own houses.

And if you are unsure of exactly how you might do this, let me remind you of another passage I read this morning, in Psalm 16:

"I will praise the Lord, who counsels me;
even at night my heart instructs me.

I keep my eyes always on the Lord.
 With him at my right hand, I will not be shaken.
Therefore my heart is glad and my tongue rejoices;
 my body also will rest secure…"
Psalm 16:7-9

Don't forget that our God counsels and instructs us – if we take time to listen, of course. And God "instructs" us in many ways, not always *(heck, not usually)* with a big flashing neon sign in the sky providing us all the answers. If God speaks, it is with a still, small voice; or with a gentle nudge; a name that pops into your head all of a sudden, or maybe in a dream *("even at night my heart instructs me")* or a certain strange desire to pick up the phone and call someone. I'd invite you to pay attention to such nudges and to act upon them, even if the person you call says: "No, I'm fine. But thanks for calling anyway."

Finally, remember, as Psalm 16 reminds us, with God "at our right hand" *(the same spot where we are told Jesus sits)* we will not be shaken *(or even stirred)* no matter what is going on in our lives and/or the world around us. We can rest secure and calm and at peace, knowing that God is with us. We might even be glad and rejoice, and find moments of worship there in our own homes, until we have the chance to rejoice and worship together again as a community of faith.

Peace be with you,

Pastor Steve

Sunday, March 29, 2020

Friends,

All of the Sunday lectionary readings today are life-affirming and hopeful in some way – a wonderful gift from God here in the midst of this anxious virus-time we find ourselves in. The first reading is Ezekiel 37:1-14, the vision Ezekiel has of a valley of dry bones:

He asked me, "Mortal, can these bones live?"
I said, "Sovereign Lord, you alone know."
Ezekiel 37:3

A valley full of dry bones hits me on a lot of levels today. There seems an obvious connection to the "valley of the shadow of death" in Psalm 23, and to a gruesome acknowledgment of how many people may eventually die worldwide, and close to home, from this Coronavirus. But also there is the perspective of some during this crisis that we'll never recover – that society won't, that our political system or voting system won't, or even that the Church, or a particular congregation won't ever recover. A community of faith that can't gather physically as community? Empty church buildings and sanctuaries - that might look like dry bones to some. Where's the life?

Indeed, as God acknowledges later in this passage:

"Mortal, these bones are the people of Israel.
They say, 'Our bones are dried up and our hope is gone; we are cut off.'"
Ezekiel 37:11

There were some people already saying that about the Church before this virus hit. Some people saying that about their particular congregations: "There's no one here anymore. Just old people. No life, no energy. Like dry bones. Our hope is gone." Notice the poignancy of that last line of complaint: "we are cut off." We're stuck at home, we're cut off from our community, cut off from friends and our church family.

But, as you know, there is great hope in this passage – the hope of the renewing power of God's Breath, the Breath of the Spirit. (*And indeed the Hebrew word "*ruah*" means both "breath" and "spirit"*) Ezekiel is instructed to tell the people that God has said "I will put my spirit within you, and you shall live" – I will breath into you and your world and your community and "you shall live." That's a spiritual promise. There is life, even when things look lifeless – even in (*especially in*) the body of Christ. What's looks dead to us is really alive.

Another of the passages in today's lectionary is John 11:1-45, the long story of the death of and subsequent raising of Lazarus by Jesus. Again, when Jesus shows up, Lazarus has been dead in the tomb four days (*one day longer than Jesus would be in the not-so-distant future*) – by all appearances, Lazarus is dead. As dead as a door nail, as dead as Jacob Marley – to all human appearances. Martha is concerned about how bad he'll smell. But then Jesus breathes on Lazarus (*OK, he shouts - but that takes breath, doesn't it?*) and Lazarus emerges from the tomb – alive and well (*and presumably with no bad odor at all*). Life brought by the breath of God where all looked lifeless and dead. Like dry bones or a corpse. Like some feel about the Church.

It all depends on the Spirit, on God's breath. That's also what the apostle Paul writes to the Romans, in another lectionary reading for this Sunday:

"The mind governed by the flesh is death,

**but the mind governed by the Spirit is life and peace…
You, however, are not in the realm of the flesh
but are in the realm of the Spirit,
if indeed the Spirit of God lives in you."**
Romans 8:6, 9

If we can let our minds be "governed" by God's Spirit (*rather than by certain politicians*) we can find life and peace, even when things look lifeless and hopeless. We have to find ways, even in the midst of a global pandemic, to let the Spirit of God live in us, and through us, and among us. We can still share God's Spirit and God's breath across distance (*God isn't constrained by space or time, so obviously God's breath isn't either*), and so even things that may look lifeless and dead right now will come back to life when all this awfulness is over. They may even come back renewed and full of new life, realizing what had been missing before that we just overlooked. Even before this crisis, I heard people voicing their opinion that the Presbyterian Church or the Church generally or their own congregation was "dead," and I always feel like responding with that famous quip of Mark Twain: "The reports of my death are greatly exaggerated." I remain very hopeful about this congregation and the Church and our world – after we get past this crisis and all the suffering and anxiety and uncertainty it brings with it.

The irony of talking about God's breath in the midst of this pandemic involving an awful respiratory disease has not escaped me. This coronavirus takes away people's breath. We are not supposed to get close enough to breathe on other people or let them breathe on us (*and for God's sake, cough into your elbow!*) Isn't it interesting that these passages about life and resurrection on this Sunday in the midst of this crisis involving a respiratory virus also involve breath as being life-giving? God is funny that way.

Finally, a word of caution in the midst of all this good news about God's life-giving Spirit and God's life-renewing breath…it doesn't come at our beck and call. Oh, sure, we have our own work to do, but we can't force God's Spirit or God's breath…we can just be open to it when it comes blowing by. Of course, we can also keep praying, too – using our breath to pray for God's breath. As the other lectionary reading for this Sunday begins:

"Out of the depths I cry to you, Lord;
    Lord, hear my voice."
Psalm 130:1

But then the Psalm goes on offer some additional advice…we should not just pray and cry out to God:

"I wait for the Lord, my whole being waits,
    and in his word I put my hope.
I wait for the Lord
    more than watchmen wait for the morning,
    more than watchmen wait for the morning.
Israel, put your hope in the Lord,
    for with the Lord is unfailing love
    and with him is full redemption."
Psalm 130:5-7

I truly believe one major aspect of praying is waiting. Waiting with hope. Waiting with faith. Waiting – trusting that God is already acting, already breathing through our world and our lives, even if we can't see evidence of it yet.

Remember, my friends, God is here. God is breathing through our world and our communities and our churches and our lives – a life-giving, life-renewing breath and Spirit – even when what we see all around us is death and disruption and disease. But no matter how dry and lifeless we may feel, no matter how out of control things may seem, as long as we are open to the breath of God and the Spirit of God (*blowing in ways we know nothing about and in places we may not even be noticing*) there is hope. Hang on to that hope, my friends, no matter what your eyes or other people or the news may tell you at any particular moment.

Peace be with you,

Pastor Steve

Wednesday, April 1, 2020

Friends,

This great reminder was part of my morning devotions earlier:

**"Therefore, since we are surrounded by so great a cloud of witnesses,
let us also lay aside every weight and the sin that clings so closely,
and let us run with perseverance the race that is set before us."**
Hebrews 12:1

What a great reminder during this time when so many are feeling lonely and isolated at home that we are (*always*) surrounded by a "great cloud of witnesses" – those who have gone before us in the faith and those who have been part of our lives and have now passed on. I think of people I have known in my previous congregations and in this one who are no longer with us, and family members – especially my grandparents – who are also no longer physical present in my life, but whose spirit and presence I can still feel at times and which gives me great comfort, even when (*especially when*) I feel all alone.

It is interesting that right after reading this reminder of the cloud of witnesses surrounding each and every one of us, I then read Psalm 34, which begins:

**"I will extol the Lord at all times;
   his praise will always be on my lips.
I will glory in the Lord;
   let the afflicted hear and rejoice.**

**Glorify the Lord with me;
   let us exalt his name together."**
Psalm 34:1-3

"Let us exalt his name together." I must admit more and more I see the irony or maybe better the poignancy of such references during this time when we cannot physically gather as a community of faith. How can we exalt God's name together when we aren't together physically? Well, maybe one of the lessons of this time of social distancing and no mass gatherings is the reminder for us that even when we are not together physically we ARE together spiritually. We ARE the body of Christ. We are the children of God. And that bond is beyond time and space. I've always sort of known that, but these days we are all learning it first-hand, and testing it to some degree. How do we stay connected spiritually when we aren't able to connect physically, with a handshake or a hug?

Also after reading the Hebrews passage about a cloud of witnesses always with us, I viewed that word "together" in an even deeper way. Because we are always surrounded by those witnesses – friends and family and fellow children of God – we are never really alone. Every time we pray or worship, even if we are all alone in our room, we are worshipping together with each other and with all those witnesses who surround us and who went before us. What a wonderful time to be reminded of that. In "normal" times (*and by that I mean up until 3 weeks ago*) it was easy to just take for granted that aspect of God's kingdom, since we were able to gather together physically (or not, if we wanted to stay in bed or get an early tee time on the golf course) – but now, when we can't gather physically, this spiritual connection between ourselves and all those who have gone before takes on added meaning and importance.

Another verse in Psalm 34 caught my eye:

> "Taste and see that the Lord is good;
> blessed is the one who takes refuge in him."

Perhaps another positive benefit of this COVID-19 pandemic and the social distancing and self-quarantining that goes with it is the savoring of other aspects of life we overlooked before, like food (*or toilet paper – but let's focus on the food, shall we?*) From what I have seen on social media, a lot of people have a lot more time on their hands now – time to cook a meal in a way they didn't before this all started. Many people aren't nearly as rushed as they were 3 weeks ago (*healthcare workers are the obvious exception, of course*) – and if you are one of them you might find you have time now to cook some recipes you haven't for a while because of time. Or, mindful of that cloud of witnesses in Hebrews 12, maybe this is the moment to pull out one of your Grandma's old recipes that you have never tried to make for yourself even though all these years you have had an old recipe card written in your Grandma's handwriting telling you how – make a batch of her gingerbread cookies or that casserole that you loved as a kid. This is both a way to honor some of the members of your cloud of witnesses, but also to take the time to enjoy taking time to cook and to eat a meal together with family (*and maybe share the stories and memories behind the recipes, too, for a new generation*).

And all of this as a way of living into another verse of this beautiful Psalm:

> "I sought the Lord, and he answered me;
> he delivered me from all my fears."
> *Psalm 34:4*

May the peace of Christ be with you all,

Pastor Steve

Saturday, April 4, 2020

Friends,
In some ways the readings in my morning devotions today seemed to be continuing the themes in yesterday's readings – especially the idea of sorrow being turned into joy, and God "returning" us to God's house and to each other.

The first reading was from the prophet Ezekiel, who was prophesying before and during the so-called Babylonian Exile of the Hebrew people (*also reflected in Psalm 137, with its poignant question: "How shall we sing the Lord's song in a strange land?"*):

"This is what the Sovereign Lord says:
I will take the Israelites out of the nations where they have gone.
I will gather them from all around and bring them back into their own land."
Ezekiel 37:21

This is a promise that the people will return to their own land, they will return to their own homes and the Temple and all that they left behind when they went into exile. But the promise is also a covenant between God and the people, that God will not desert them (and perhaps the hope that they will not desert God again, either):

"My dwelling place will be with them;
I will be their God, and they will be my people.
Then the nations will know that I the Lord make Israel holy, when my sanctuary is among them forever."
Ezekiel 37:27-28

Notice, God will dwell with them (*even though God was already dwelling with them, even there in Babylon, but God is making this explicit promise so they won't fear the future when their crisis is over and they return to their homeland*) and, this is the line that really caught my attention: "my sanctuary is among them forever." Even when we can't gather for worship in our sanctuary here at First Presbyterian Church, God is with us in the sanctuary of each of our lives. God's true sanctuary is not a room in a church building, but in each of our hearts. God is our God and we are God's people (*all of us, every single human being*).

God WILL bring us back together, of course. That was part of God's promise to the Hebrew people during their exile and it is, I believe, just as much God's promise to us during our "exile" from each other and from gathered worship. This idea was reinforced in another of my readings this morning, from another prophet who was speaking God's Word during the period of the Babylonian Exile:

"**Hear the word of the Lord, you nations;**
    proclaim it in distant coastlands:
'**He who scattered Israel will gather them**
    and will watch over his flock like a shepherd.'
For the Lord will deliver Jacob
    and redeem them from the hand of those stronger
than they.
They will come and shout for joy on the heights of Zion;
    they will rejoice in the bounty of the Lord—
the grain, the new wine and the olive oil,
    the young of the flocks and herds.
They will be like a well-watered garden,
    and they will sorrow no more.

> Then young women will dance and be glad,
>   young men and old as well.
> I will turn their mourning into gladness;
>   I will give them comfort and joy instead of sorrow."
Jeremiah 31:10-13

God is a God who sometimes scatters God's people, but God is also a God what gathers them back together. And when this COVID-19 crisis is over *(or at least subsided)* and we are able to return to some sort of "normalcy," God will turn sorrow in joy and we will rejoice. Don't miss the amazing image that Jeremiah uses to describe the people after they return to God and to each other, when they are able to once again rejoice in the bounty of the Lord: "They will be like a well-watered garden, and they will sorrow no more." I'm not sure I've ever stopped to consider how blessed and content a well-watered garden must feel, but that's the joy and contentment and peace that is promised to us. Just a week ago I planted some apple trees I had gotten from our local county extension office, and every time I water them from now on, I am going to think about this image from Jeremiah *(and also that image from Psalm 1 which describes those who trust in God as being like trees).*

Finally, let me just lift up another of my morning readings, the beautiful and comforting Psalm 121:

> "I lift up my eyes to the mountains—
>   where does my help come from?
> My help comes from the Lord,
>   the Maker of heaven and earth.
> He will not let your foot slip –
> he who watches over you will not slumber;
> indeed, he who watches over Israel will neither slumber nor sleep.

The Lord watches over you—
>   the Lord is your shade at your right hand;
> the sun will not harm you by day,
>   nor the moon by night.
> The Lord will keep you from all harm—
>   he will watch over your life;
> the Lord will watch over your coming and going
>   both now and forevermore."

Psalm 121

I love this entire Psalm (*it is one of those Psalms that, as I read it, I can almost feel my blood pressure dropping and my body relaxing*) but especially, in this moment of time, the reminder that "the Lord will watch over your coming and going, both now and forevermore." Of course, many of us are not doing nearly as much coming and going as we were doing just a few weeks ago (*and that's OK – STAY HOME and STAY SAFE!*) but when we do venture out for necessities, isn't it nice to know that the Lord watches over us? And that when we finally are able to come back out and go into the church sanctuary together without any fear or concern for our health or the health of those around us, the Lord will be watching over us then, too. With a smile.

Until we gather again, may peace be with you.

Pastor Steve

Friday, April 17, 2020

Friends,

As part of my morning devotions for the past few weeks I have been reading through the book of Exodus (*I'm up to Exodus 14 as of this morning, just before the Red Sea parts*). I must admit, it has been a little bizarre to be reading about all the plagues during this virus crisis.

One of the other things I have been reminded of in Exodus is how often Pharaoh says he will let Moses and Aaron and the Hebrew people leave, and then changes his mind. But Exodus never really says that Pharaoh changes his mind, it says again and again "his heart was hardened."

I'm going to leave aside the fact that in places Exodus says that God hardened Pharaoh's heart, because at other times it says that Pharaoh hardened his own heart. This to me seems much more likely – that at times we, like Pharaoh, let our hearts get hardened: clenched, unyielding, stony.

Indeed, there are many verses of the Bible that warn against this happening.

Hebrews 3:8, for example, warns:

> **"do not harden your hearts as in the rebellion, as on the day of testing in the wilderness."**

Notice that the writer of Hebrews implies that Pharaoh's heart isn't the only one that gets hardened in the Exodus story – the Hebrew people, once they get into the wilderness and start grumbling and complaining, also experience hard hearts.

And lest we think hard heartedness was simply an Old Testament problem, let me remind you of what Mark's gospel says about the disciples after Jesus feeds the five thousand and then comes walking out to them in their boat on the Sea of Galilee and calms the rough water:

**"They were completely amazed,
for they had not understood about the loaves;
their hearts were hardened."**
Mark 6:51-52

Somehow a hard heart is related to misunderstanding Jesus. We need soft hearts to receive what Jesus tries to tell us and teach us.

And a soft heart is also necessary for obeying, not just receiving, God's Word. When God was speaking to (*and through*) Ezekiel about how God would restore Israel (*after the Babylonian exile*), God declared that:

**"I will give them an undivided heart and put a new spirit in them;
I will remove from them their heart of stone and give them a heart of flesh.
Then they will follow my decrees and be careful to keep my laws.
They will be my people, and I will be their God."**
Ezekiel 11:19-20

God doesn't like cold, hard hearts – God wants our hearts to be soft and warm and overflowing with love. Our God who can produce water out of a rock finds it even harder to produce love out of a cold, hard heart.

Indeed, there is even a pretty dire warning in the book of Romans about how we will be judged by God if we let our hearts get hardened by disobedience and sin:

**"But by your hard and impenitent heart
you are storing up wrath for yourself on the day of wrath,
when God's righteous judgment will be revealed."**
Romans 2:5

There are many other places in the Bible that warn against letting our hearts get hard and unloving and cold, but I want to move on to mention why this seems of particular importance for us to hear in these difficult and uncertain times. Because it is in difficult and uncertain times that we especially need to try to keep our hearts from getting hard and unloving, because the temptation is even greater than normal. Fear is one of the main causes of a hard heart.

Love is the opposite of fear *(it even "casts out fear," according to 1 John)*, and we all need to be loved and be loving in times such as these, as best we can. When I hear or read comments about how opening up the economy is worth a certain amount of loss of life *("only 2-3%")* I sense that I am hearing from a heart that has grown a little hard. When I see Christian churches still gathering, risking the spread of a deadly virus, I have to wonder if there are some stony hearts amongst the leadership of that church. When I see people ignoring requests to stay at home and stay six feet apart and wear masks when in public *(for the sake of others, not yourself)* I have to wonder if this is an outward sign of a heart that is growing chilly and hard.

Look, we are all struggling in these difficult times. And love is difficult even in the best of times, and it can be even harder these days. But that's why, as followers of Jesus Christ (*who had the softest, warmest, most loving heart any human has ever had*) need to do our best, go out of our way, to be as loving and caring and compassionate as we can possibly be.

Friends, don't let your hearts get hardened by bad news or fear or uncertainty. Keep your hearts soft by expressing love and showing respect and refraining from too much judgmentalism. And be sure to extend that love to yourself as well – take care of yourself so you can help take care of others.

Friends – stay well, keep your hearts as soft as you can, and may the peace of Christ and the love of God be with you,

Pastor Steve

Saturday, April 18, 2020

Friends,

I began my day with Psalm 116, the first reading in today's daily lectionary. And, as often happens, one particular verse jumped out at me:

How can I repay the Lord for all the good He has done for me?
Psalm 116:12

Some translations ask: "What can I return to the Lord?" or "What shall I render to the Lord?" but the idea is the same in all these translations – God has been so very good to us *(far beyond what any of us deserve – and even in the midst of a global pandemic)* that it is unclear how we can – if we can – ever repay that goodness or return it to God in any way.

And of course the obvious answer is: we can't. We can never repay God for all God's goodness; we can never return to God more than the tiniest, most miniscule, fraction of that goodness. But…that doesn't mean we shouldn't try.

I believe there are two basic ways we can begin to repay or return to God the goodness God showers upon us each and every day. The first way is to offer prayer and praise to God directly, and the second way is to repay that goodness to God by showing goodness to other people.

The first part of repaying God is well documented in another of my readings this morning, the wonderful Psalm 150:

"Praise the Lord.

Praise God in his sanctuary;
  praise him in his mighty heavens.
Praise him for his acts of power;
  praise him for his surpassing greatness.
Praise him with the sounding of the trumpet,
  praise him with the harp and lyre,
praise him with timbrel and dancing,
  praise him with the strings and pipe,
praise him with the clash of cymbals,
  praise him with resounding cymbals.

Let everything that has breath praise the Lord.
Praise the Lord."

So there you have it – we can repay God by praising God. And notice how this Psalm describes for us the where, why, how, and who of such praise.

We are to praise God in God's sanctuary, which is not bound by the physical limits of our church sanctuary, or any church building, but is indeed the entire universe: "his mighty heavens".

Why are we to praise God? Not just for God's goodness, mentioned in Psalm 116, but for God's "acts of power" and for God's "surpassing greatness"(*God is both "great" and "good"*).

How are we to praise God? In many different ways, but according to this Psalm mostly through music: trumpets, harps, lyres, timbrels (*a timbrel was an ancient percussion instrument similar to a tambourine*), stringed instruments, pipes (*which I take to mean what we call "wind" instruments like clarinets and saxophones, but maybe*

God especially likes bagpipes – my Scottish ancestors would certainly approve of that interpretation as well), and cymbals – clashing and resounding cymbals. Music is obviously one of God's favorite forms of praise.

And finally, this Psalm reminds us who is supposed to praise God: "everything that has breath." In other words, pretty much all of creation – all humans, all birds, all creatures (*including our pets*), all fish, and I think we could even include plants (*photosynthesis is akin to breathing*). So no creature is excluded from the set of those who should praise God.

I also believe we can repay God for all God's goodness by being good to other creatures and other human beings. Remember what the king tells the people at the moment of judgment pictured in Matthew's gospel:

**"Truly I tell you,
whatever you did for one of the least of these brothers and sisters of mine,
you did for me."**
Matthew 25:40

By being good to others, by showing kindness and compassion and consideration to others, we are in a sense showing that goodness and kindness and compassion and consideration to God, and that is another way to return to God the goodness God has shown (*and continues to show*) us.

There's another thing about goodness, too – it is contagious. I came across a verse in the book of Acts this morning, in the story of the religious authorities trying to stop Peter and John from preaching about Jesus and healing people in the name of Jesus, which I must admit, in this time of COVID-19, hit me like a thunderbolt. This is what the religious authorities say to themselves as they are deliberating how to react to what Peter and John and the other disciples are saying and doing:

"But to stop this thing from spreading any further among the people,
we must warn them to speak no longer to anyone in this name."
Acts 4:17

Goodness is contagious. It spreads – like a virus. You touch one person's life in a good way, and then they pass that along, and soon goodness and love are spreading everywhere. Unfortunately, we humans and our societies have developed a lot of vaccines against goodness – rules and regulations and roadblocks and hardened hearts (*see yesterday's email*). But if we could, each one of us, try to share some goodness and love with at least one other person each and every day – well, the result would be a global pandemic of goodness and love that hopefully everyone would eventually catch.

Friends – in these difficult times, do the best you can to spread love instead of COVID-19.

Stay well, and may the peace of Christ and the love of God continue to surround you!

Pastor Steve

Thursday, May 7, 2020

Friends,

One of my Scripture readings this morning was the story of Moses going back up to Mount Sinai to get a replacement copy of the Ten Commandments after the whole Golden Calf incident (*during which Moses smashed the original stone tablets, ground them into dust, sprinkled them in water, and made the people drink it – in case you had forgotten*). Anyway, when Moses comes back down from Mount Sinai this time, we get this interesting conclusion:

"Moses came down from Mount Sinai. As he came down from the mountain with the two covenant tablets in his hand, Moses didn't realize that the skin of his face shone brightly because he had been talking with God. When Aaron and all the Israelites saw the skin of Moses' face shining brightly, they were afraid to come near him. But Moses called them closer. So Aaron and all the leaders of the community came back to him, and Moses spoke with them. After that, all the Israelites came near as well, and Moses commanded them everything that the Lord had spoken with him on Mount Sinai. When Moses finished speaking with them, he put a veil over his face. Whenever Moses went into the Lord's presence to speak with him, Moses would take the veil off until he came out again. When Moses came out and told the Israelites what he had been commanded, the Israelites would see that the skin of Moses' face was shining brightly. So Moses would put the veil on his face again until the next time he went in to speak with the Lord."
Exodus 34:29-35

I have read this story many times before, but what struck me in reading it here in this time of COVID-19 was the similarities between the veil Moses put on his face and the masks so many of us (*it should be ALL of us – hint, hint*) are wearing.

First of all, notice that Moses puts on this veil for the benefit of the other people, not for his own benefit. They are scared by the radiance of his face after he meets with God, shining with the reflection of the divine light. Perhaps this reminded them of their own failings when it came to their relationship with God (*and knowing the Israelites, they probably grumbled and complained until Moses gave in, too*). But, in order not to "infect" the people with fear because of his shining face, Moses began wearing a veil whenever he wasn't speaking to God.

This is pretty similar to the reason we all should be wearing masks when we are out in public and around other people these days: for the benefit of others. A mask may not do that much to protect the person wearing it, but it can do a whole lot to keep that person from infecting everyone else. Moses was wise enough to know that even though he wasn't bothered by his face shining with God's light, if it bothered other people, he should wear that veil. So it is with wearing a mask. Do it for others, like Moses did with his veil.

And I'll bet Moses was uncomfortable wearing that veil, too. It was probably making his glasses steam up and hurting his ears and making it harder to talk to other people – but he did it just the same, because he cared about the people around him.

This story of Moses also reveals the utter ridiculousness of comments from people like Ohio State Representative Nino Vitale who said recently on Facebook that he would not be wearing a mask because everyone is made in the image of God (*especially our faces*) and God would not want us to cover that up. I can almost hear Moses pulling out his hair AND his beard hearing that…

Folks, above all else God wants us to care about and take care of other people, and to think about others as much as we think about ourselves *("love your neighbor as yourself")*, so I feel pretty confident in assuring you that God will not be angry if you take the sensible public health step of wearing a mask when you are around other people. In fact, I think God would probably give you a gold star or something for making the effort on behalf of your fellow human beings.

So please wear a mask. And when you do, maybe think about Moses wearing that veil, and know that you are in very good company.

And may the peace of Christ and the love of God continue to be with each and every one of you.

Pastor Steve

Tuesday, May 12, 2020

Friends,

I've been reading through the story of Moses and the Israelites as part of my morning lectionary. Well, that narrative has moved from Exodus into Numbers now, and this morning I read the fascinating *(and I think timely – but I'll say more about that in a minute!)* story that is told in Numbers, chapter 11.

This occurs in the second year the people have been in the wilderness, and up to this point they have been surviving on the manna that God was sending every day *(except on the Sabbath)*. The Israelites, despite this heavenly food sent directly from God, begin to grumble and complain:

"The rabble among them began to crave other food, and again the Israelites started wailing and said, "If only we had meat to eat! We remember the fish we ate in Egypt at no cost—also the cucumbers, melons, leeks, onions and garlic. But now we have lost our appetite; we never see anything but this manna!"
Numbers 11:4-6

Now I am sure none of you are grumbling about life right now about things you miss from before COVID-19 and stay-at-home orders; I'm sure no one is complaining about not being able to eat in restaurants or get their hair cut or anything like that…but, maybe we can sympathize a little bit with the Israelites, who, after well over a year, have only had manna to eat *(even though Exodus tells us that it tasted like "wafers made with honey" and Numbers 11:8 says the manna tasted like "cakes baked with oil")*. The Israelites were getting tired of this routine, they were getting tired of each day being just like the one before, at least in terms of their diet. They were ready to move on, to get to the Promised Land, to be done with this wilderness-thing and this manna-menu and get back to normal life.

Now the first thing God does is tell Moses to pick seventy men that he trusts and bring them to the Tent of Meeting and God will bestow a portion of the Spirit on them so they can help Moses bear the burden of all this grumbling and complaining. Then God tells Moses to tell the people this:

"Tell the people: 'Consecrate yourselves in preparation for tomorrow, when you will eat meat. The Lord heard you when you wailed, "If only we had meat to eat! We were better off in Egypt!" Now the Lord will give you meat, and you will eat it. You will not eat it for just one day, or two days, or five, ten or twenty days, but for a whole month—until it comes out of your nostrils and you loathe it—because you have rejected the Lord, who is among you, and have wailed before him, saying, "Why did we ever leave Egypt?"'"
Numbers 11:18-20

That's very much God's style, at least in the Old Testament. You want meat? Ok, I'll give you meat, so much meat that you'll gorge yourselves and meat will be coming out your nostrils and you'll hate it and maybe realize how stupid you were to complain about the manna *(this is akin to what God will do centuries later when the people of Israel demand that Samuel find them a king – Samuel tries to warn them that a king will take away all their rights, but they insist, and God says, in essence, "OK, I'll give them what they want – their loss.")*. So:

"Now a wind went out from the Lord and drove quail in from the sea. It scattered them up to two cubits *(about 3*

feet) **deep all around the camp, as far as a day's walk in any direction. All that day and night and all the next day the people went out and gathered quail.** No one gathered less than ten homers *(about 1.6 metric tons)*. **Then they spread them out all around the camp. But while the meat was still between their teeth and before it could be consumed, the anger of the Lord burned against the people, and he struck them with a severe plague. Therefore the place was named Kibroth Hattaavah, because there they buried the people who had craved other food."**
Numbers 11:31-34

Kibroth Hattaavah, by the way, literally means: "graves of craving."

I can't help wondering if there might be a lesson for us here in this odd story, a warning perhaps about how we as a society and a nation and even a world respond to the effects of COVID-19.

There is a desire, a "craving" even, to open things back up quickly, to get back to normal *(remember how good life was in February, back in Egypt?)*. We're tired of being stuck at home, we're tired of businesses being closed, we're tired of not being able to gather for worship and social activities and sporting events. But there is a huge risk if we let our desire for getting back to normal and our craving for the way things used to be blind us to the dangers of doing so too quickly, before public health officials believe we are ready and prepared to do so as a society.

My fear is we create a modern Kibroth Hattaavah with "graves of craving" – people who will die because some others were craving an end to staying at home and social distancing and wearing masks and not being able to get haircuts and eat at restaurants and gather in churches. As I mentioned in an email last week about wearing masks, I truly believe that what God most cares about is love and how we treat each other; if we have to grit our teeth and keep staying at home a while longer and not give into our craving for a quick return to "normal life", then I truly believe God is in favor of us doing that, thinking about more than just ourselves.

We humans are never good at this. None of us really likes being patient and selfless and bored and scared and all the things we may be experiencing right now. But it seems like it is about time, after thousands of years, for us to learn to do better than the Israelites (*and so many after them*) did…to put aside our grumbling and complaining and craving for something different (*or a return to what we once knew in Egypt, at least the good things we remember*) and try to keep doing our best to stay put and wear masks and keep our distance and support each other and love each other and help each other get through all this together. Let's not experience another Kibroth Hattaavah.

May the peace of Christ and the love of God continue to be with you in these trying times.
Pastor Steve

Wednesday, May 20, 2020

Friends,

Today's email will be short but hopefully sweet *(if it is possible for something to be "sweet" in a challenging way)*. Among my Scripture readings this morning was this short passage from the Letter to the Colossians. As I read it…and then reread it…a possible title for this passage began to form in my mind: "How God Wishes We'd Behave During a Global Pandemic":

"Therefore, as God's chosen people, holy and dearly loved, clothe yourselves with compassion, kindness, humility, gentleness and patience. Bear with each other and forgive one another if any of you has a grievance against someone. Forgive as the Lord forgave you. And over all these virtues put on love, which binds them all together in perfect unity.

Let the peace of Christ rule in your hearts, since as members of one body you were called to peace. And be thankful."
Colossians 3:12-15

There's a lot of information out there these days, a lot of tips on what to do about COVID-19 and what to do to keep your kids entertained and yourself sane while staying at home and what to do when out in public. Colossians offers a pretty good basic summary of what we, as followers of Christ, ought to do in addition to all that: be compassionate, kind, humble, gentle, patient, forbearing, forgiving, loving and thankful. Oh, and let the peace of Christ rule in our hearts, too.

There you go. Simple, right? Until you start trying to put it into practice.

I'd suggest starting with one or two of those suggestions rather than trying to do all of them all at once. These days, it can be a struggle to simply try to be compassionate or gentle or patient, much less all of that at once. AND to be thankful. AND to be loving. AND to be forgiving. Wow, might as well just go back to bed right now and call it a day…

But as with all such suggestions in Scripture, I truly believe God gives us credit for trying - for the attempt - even if (*and when*) we fall short. So I'd suggest writing or printing out these verses from Colossians and putting them somewhere you can refer to them often – in your Bible or taped to your bathroom mirror or maybe posted on the forehead of everyone else in your household. The point is to try to live this way more and more, as best we can, especially when this pandemic seems to be bringing out the worst qualities and behaviors in too many people. Let's do our best to rise about that and work on being better followers of Christ. We won't ever reach perfection in living out all those values listed in these verses, but we can always do better. And…not to brag or anything, but I managed to be a little bit patient the other day for about 4 ½ minutes, so it IS possible (*I'm going to shoot for a full 5 minutes of patience sometime next week after I'm fully recovered from this week's effort*).

Finally, this list in Colossians will actually serve us well ALL the time, not just in these especially difficult, disruptive and uncertain times. Indeed, it can sometimes be even harder to be loving and patient and gentle and such when life seems to be going well.

So maybe I'll rethink the title I gave today's passage: "How God Wishes We'd Behave During a Global Pandemic…And At All Other Times, Too."

May the peace of Christ and the love of God continue to uplift you.

Pastor Steve

Saturday, June 13, 2020

Friends,

I'm just going to jump right into today's passage:

"When Jesus had finished speaking, a Pharisee invited him to eat with him; so he went in and reclined at the table. But the Pharisee was surprised when he noticed that Jesus did not first wash before the meal.

Then the Lord said to him, "Now then, you Pharisees clean the outside of the cup and dish, but inside you are full of greed and wickedness. You foolish people! Did not the one who made the outside make the inside also? But now as for what is inside you—be generous to the poor, and everything will be clean for you.

"Woe to you Pharisees, because you give God a tenth of your mint, rue and all other kinds of garden herbs, but you neglect justice and the love of God. You should have practiced the latter without leaving the former undone.

"Woe to you Pharisees, because you love the most important seats in the synagogues and respectful greetings in the marketplaces.

"Woe to you, because you are like unmarked graves, which people walk over without knowing it."

One of the experts in the law answered him, "Teacher, when you say these things, you insult us also."

Jesus replied, "And you experts in the law, woe to you, because you load people down with burdens they can hardly carry, and you yourselves will not lift one finger to help them."
Luke 11:37-46

First of all, ever since I was ordained as a pastor in June, 1997, I have read such references to the Pharisees in a different light than I did before being ordained. Before that I just assumed the Pharisees were the "bad guys" and then one day after becoming a pastor I realized that I had become, literally, a Pharisee, at least in the sense of being a religious leader, an official part of the institutional church. That made me pause and ask myself: "AM I a Pharisee?"

I think it is often too easy for all of us to simply dismiss the Pharisees as "them," the "bad guys" who didn't see (*as we obviously all would have if we had been living back then*) who Jesus really was.

But notice what Jesus is accusing the Pharisees of doing in this passage – paying more attention to surface appearances than to underlying reality – hypocrisy, in essence. And aren't we all guilty of that, at least sometimes?

Of course I couldn't help but think of the initial reference to hand-washing here in this time of COVID-19. Hand-washing was a religious ritual for the Pharisees, as it is quickly becoming for many of us in a sense these days (*and you SHOULD wash your hands religiously...even to the extent of singing a whole hymn while doing so to make sure you are washing them long enough*). But the point Jesus makes is that washing the outside doesn't do anything to defeat the germs of hate and fear and greed and such that we have on the inside.

So if you are washing your hands and wearing a mask to protect yourself and other people, but you are also treating other people badly...well, you just might be a Pharisee. If you are pointing fingers at others for not remembering the least among us, but not being generous to the poor yourself...well, you just might be a Pharisee. If you cry out about other people, protesters maybe, for breaking the law but you yourself have been known to drive over the speed limit or ignore a stop sign or fudge a bit on your income taxes...well, you just might be a Pharisee. If you claim to be a follower of Jesus Christ but you ridicule "those people" who aren't living their lives just the way you do and don't go the same church as you do or vote the same way you do...well, you just might be a Pharisee. If you claim to be better than the Pharisees...well, you just might be a Pharisee.

To paraphrase that great comic strip POGO: "We have met the Pharisees – and they are us."

Especially during these strange, unusual, difficult, disruptive, stressful, scary times in which we are living, I think we all need to go out of our way to make sure we are not being judgmental and hypocritical (*and just plain critical*) like the Pharisees were being in the time of Jesus. This is a good time to go out of our way to make sure before we criticize anyone else for anything (*a speck or two perhaps*) that we aren't worthy of a little criticism ourselves (*I'd write more but I have this log in my eye making it difficult to see to type*).

Maybe this is a good time to commit (*or recommit yet again for some of us*) to being a little bit less like the Pharisees and a little bit more like Jesus...as best we can.

Friends, may the peace of Christ and the love of God not only be with you today, but flow out of you to enrich other people's lives through you as well.

Pastor Steve

Wednesday, June 17

Friends,

Have you ever worried about anything? (*If not, you are excused from today's reflection*)

If so, do you find yourself worrying more in recent days/weeks/months?

Boy, have I got the Scripture passage for you!

"Then Jesus said to his disciples, "Therefore, I say to you, don't worry about your life, what you will eat, or about your body, what you will wear. There is more to life than food and more to the body than clothing. Consider the ravens: they neither plant nor harvest, they have no silo or barn, yet God feeds them. You are worth so much more than birds! Who among you by worrying can add a single moment to your life? If you can't do such a small thing, why worry about the rest? Notice how the lilies grow. They don't wear themselves out with work, and they don't spin cloth. But I say to you that even Solomon in all his splendor wasn't dressed like one of these. If God dresses grass in the field so beautifully, even though it's alive today and tomorrow it's thrown into the furnace, how much more will God do for you, you people of weak faith! Don't chase after what you will eat and what you will drink. Stop worrying. All the nations of the world long for these things. Your Father knows that you need them.

Instead, desire his kingdom and these things will be given to you as well."
Luke 12:22-31

See how easy it is? Just don't worry. Stop worrying.

Unfortunately, trying not to worry is a bit like trying to make yourself fall asleep – the harder you try, the further away from your goal you get. And then you start worrying about how much trouble you're having trying not to worry. And so on...

And yet the logic here is sound. Why DO we worry? Worrying doesn't solve anything, it doesn't solve a single issue that we may be worrying about. It just makes things worse, really. I try telling myself that when I am wide awake at 3:00am worrying about something (*usually something fairly minor, too – it is the little things that tend to take up the most space in my personal worry schedule*) but it doesn't usually help.

I did a little research and came across some interesting ideas about why we worry:

"When we have a hard time living with this uncertainty, we might return to the situation in our mind and keep turning it over, imaging every "what if" and how we might handle it—we're trying to control an uncontrollable situation. Worrying about uncertain future events reinforces itself.

How can a mental state tied to so much anxiety be rewarding? Each time we worry and nothing bad happens, our mind connects worry with preventing harm:

worry = nothing bad happens.

And the takeaway is, "It's a good thing I worried." (We probably aren't consciously aware of this thought process.)"
[this is from the website of "Psychology Today" magazine]

Author James Clear offers this reflection about why we worry:

"Most of the choices you make today will not benefit you immediately. If you do a good job at work today, you'll get a paycheck in a few weeks. If you save money now, you'll have enough for retirement later. Many aspects of modern society are designed to delay rewards until some point in the future.

This is true of our problems as well. While a giraffe is worried about immediate problems like avoiding lions and seeking shelter from a storm, many of the problems humans worry about are problems of the future."

Because the things we often worry about are in the future, and we live in a "Delayed Return Environment," we have lots of time to worry about problems that may not resolve themselves for a long time, giving us even more time to worry – much more than that giraffe that James Clear mentions.

In addition, the giraffe worries about problems it has some measure of control over – avoiding lions, for example. The giraffe knows places where lions generally are, and the giraffe can avoid them, or travel in a group (*a group of giraffes is called a "tower" – I looked it up*).

We face issues, many of which are in the future (*and have a delayed or indeterminate resolution period*) or out of our control (*or at least seemingly out of our control*) and so we feel helpless. And so we worry. And if nothing bad happens, we are reinforced in our often unconscious believe that somehow our worrying helped things turn out OK.

So all of this is perfectly natural and even rational, to some degree. But that doesn't make it healthy or productive or joyful.

That's where Jesus comes in. Jesus knows all this (*and more!*) – Jesus knows what it is to be human and to feel stress and to worry, but Jesus also knows about God, and that's who he's trying to remind us about in today's passage. There's an alternative to worrying when we feel stressed or anxious or helpless or uncertain; one might say there are vaccines against it.

There is prayer, for one thing. We can always take control of what worries us by praying about it. We can even pray about being worried. And, we should never worry about praying, either – as the Nike ad says: Just do it. There are no rules to worry about when it comes to prayer, no right or wrong way to pray – just pray in whatever way you feel you need to or want to – sometimes you might even use words.

Another vaccine against worry is seeking or desiring God's kingdom, by which I think Jesus means always be looking for ways to share the values of God's kingdom – love, peace, joy, hope, forgiveness, justice – with others and be looking for how others are sharing them with you. How we live in the world and how we respond to others IS something we can control.

So when we feel like there are so many things that are out of our control, we can always do something to bring peace and love and hope to someone else. Even just a phone call or a card or a smile – SOMETHING, some gesture of God's kingdom shared with another person. THAT we can always do. Will that solve all our problems? Nope. But it might be the very solution for someone else and doing that will at least take our mind off our own problems for a moment. And, unlike worrying, sharing love and hope and peace with someone else won't make our problems any worse.

I try to practice what I preach in this regard, but I'll be honest – I usually fail miserably. But I'm not going to worry about that – I'm just going to keep trying!

Friends, may the peace of Christ and the love of God be with you today, and may you find a way to share some of that peace and love *(and joy and hope, etc.)* with someone else today, too.

No worries.

Pastor Steve

Friday, July 10, 2020

Friends,

I think I have found the "perfect" COVID-19 (*or 2020*) Psalm:

LORD, you are the God who saves me;
  day and night I cry out to you.
May my prayer come before you;
  turn your ear to my cry.
I am overwhelmed with troubles
  and my life draws near to death.
I am counted among those who go down to the pit;
  I am like one without strength.
I am set apart with the dead,
  like the slain who lie in the grave,
whom you remember no more,
  who are cut off from your care.
You have put me in the lowest pit,
  in the darkest depths.
Your wrath lies heavily on me;
  you have overwhelmed me with all your waves.
You have taken from me my closest friends
  and have made me repulsive to them.
I am confined and cannot escape;
  my eyes are dim with grief.
I call to you, LORD, every day;
  I spread out my hands to you.
Do you show your wonders to the dead?
  Do their spirits rise up and praise you?
Is your love declared in the grave,
  your faithfulness in Destruction?
Are your wonders known in the place of darkness,
  or your righteous deeds in the land of oblivion?

But I cry to you for help, LORD;
  in the morning my prayer comes before you.
Why, LORD, do you reject me
  and hide your face from me?
From my youth I have suffered and been close to death;
  I have borne your terrors and am in despair.
Your wrath has swept over me;
  your terrors have destroyed me.
All day long they surround me like a flood;
  they have completely engulfed me.
You have taken from me friend and neighbor—
  darkness is my closest friend.
Psalm 88

In the past I have noted in my Bible that this seems the "perfect" depression Psalm, too – it certainly reflects my experience in that regard.

But now it also seems like it may get to what many of us are feeling in terms of this time of COVID-19 (*and protests and economic troubles and all of that as well – the whole mix of 2020*).

For one thing, I know that I have been doing a lot more praying, especially in the sense of crying out to God, day and night. And even problems and issues that I know are minor, even trivial, seem to loom large (*especially in the middle of the night when I can't sleep*).

I'm not sure we really are, either as individuals or as a society, in the "lowest pit" and the "darkest depths," but sometimes it can sure feel that way.

The verse: *"You have taken from me my closest friends"* also hits home in this time of self-quarantine and social distancing, when many of us are missing being physically present with friends and family. And then the Psalm adds: *"I am confined and cannot escape"* – how's that for a summation of the feeling of self-quarantine after 3+ months?

And I suspect there may be many people wondering where God is in all the turmoil of our current world. Has God rejected us? Has God hidden God's face from us? Is this God's wrath sweeping over us? *(This Psalm doesn't answer those questions, so, based on other passages of the Bible, let me confidently answer them, in order:* No, No, and No.*)*

Finally, I don't know if this Psalm was any inspiration to Paul Simon when he wrote the song "The Sound of Silence" back in the 1960s, but I can't read the final verse *("darkness is my closest friend")* without thinking of the beginning of that song: "Hello darkness, my old friend" – in fact I have those words penciled next to this verse in my Bible.

So what do you think? Can we declare Psalm 88 the official COVID-19 Psalm?

If nothing else, this Psalm reminds us that many of the thoughts and feelings we have right now are nothing new – human beings have been thinking and feeling this way in the face of turmoil and uncertainty for thousands of years, maybe since day one. So if you are feeling any of these things, you are not alone – in fact, you are in good company.

Friends, may the peace of Christ and the love of God continue to uphold you.

Pastor Steve

Thursday, July 23, 2020

Friends,

The first Bible passage I read this morning was Psalm 143, which includes this verse:

"Teach me to do your will,
   for you are my God;
may your good Spirit
   lead me on level ground."
Psalm 143:10

Nineteen weeks ago, I might have just passed right on by this verse.

Nineteen weeks ago I was still able to go to the local fitness center and work out, which I did most days. Then came COVID-19. With the fitness center shut down, I started running outside for exercise.

I am not a runner (*although I come from a family chock full of them*). I have run a 5K race twice in my life (*once when I was a teenager*). So beginning to run outdoors for exercise was a change. For one thing, it created new aches and pains in parts of my body that didn't used to hurt from time spent on the elliptical machine at the fitness center. For another, I suddenly started paying a lot more attention to the weather, since I was outside running in it (*or finding excuses NOT to run in it*).

On the plus side, I have gotten to know the flora and fauna and people living on Byrd Branch Road quite well, and I now recognize people by their vehicles as they drive by and wave to me (*it wouldn't surprise me if I am known by the people along Byrd*

Branch as *"that weird guy who runs"*). I have gotten to know (*or at least be greeted by barks from*) all the neighborhood dogs.

Running has not gotten an easier in the past nineteen weeks. In fact, some days it seems even harder. I have discovered that going out and running is a bit like going out into the world of daily life every day. Some days seem easy, and you glide along without even realizing it. Other days are a tough slog, when every step takes a certain effort of will.

But I have also learned this lesson, which I think applies to both running and life: just keep going. You may run a little slower, you may even have to walk for a stretch, but keep putting one foot in front of the other, keep taking one more step, and then another, and eventually you will have finished your run (*for that day*). I have come to appreciate even more those words of the apostle Paul written to his friend and colleague Timothy: *"I have fought the good fight, I have finished the race, I have kept the faith."*

It also amazes me how many little hills there are along Byrd Branch Road that I never noticed before when driving in my car. Growing up in the relatively flat Midwest, the few times I have "run" in the past it has usually been on flat, level ground. I THOUGHT Byrd Branch was pretty flat and level…until I started running it. Some days the ascent doesn't seem too bad, but other days I am honestly not sure if I am going to make it to my turnaround point (*just past the Byrd Branch Baptist Church – a mile and a half up the hill from Jack's Creek*). Again, this is how some days of my life feel, too – wondering if I am going to make it.

All of this is why Psalm 143:10 jumped out at me today. And reminded me of this verse from the prophet Isaiah:

> "Every valley shall be lifted up,
>   and every mountain and hill be made low;
> the uneven ground shall become level,
>   and the rough places a plain."

Isaiah 40:4

After nineteen weeks of running, "level ground" sounds wonderful, almost like paradise (*I ran a couple days recently when I was back visiting my hometown in northwest Ohio – where it is FLAT and LEVEL – and it almost felt like I was taking a nap instead of running, that's how much easier it was than running on Byrd Branch*).

Level ground does not wear you out. The "running" is easy (*like the "yoke" that Jesus promises us in Matthew 11:30*). With God, the living is easy, too – at least compared to trying to live without God. God promises to level out the rough places and the difficult hills on our path, at least spiritually. Running through life with God is akin to those days when I realize I've made it to my turn around point and I still have energy left, it didn't seem TOO bad, I know I'll be able to make it back home with no problem.

Anyway, that's how this one verse in Psalm 143 struck me today. As a reminder of how God helps make our daily run of life easier than it might otherwise have been. We still have to run it, and we may even have some hills to climb, but God will help level them out somehow and help us find the energy to keep putting one foot in front of the other.

Friends, may the leveling love of God and the peace of Christ be with you this day, whatever road you may be running in your life.

Pastor Steve

Friday, July 24, 2020

Friends,

This is one of those days when nothing really jumped off the page at me during my morning devotions. But these famous words from Shakespeare's **Macbeth** HAVE been swirling around in my head all week:

**"Tomorrow, and tomorrow, and tomorrow,
Creeps in this petty pace from day to day,
To the last syllable of recorded time;
And all our yesterdays have lighted fools
The way to dusty death. Out, out, brief candle!
Life's but a walking shadow, a poor player,
That struts and frets his hour upon the stage,
And then is heard no more. It is a tale
Told by an idiot, full of sound and fury,
Signifying nothing."**
Macbeth, Act 5, Scene 5

This soliloquy gets to the heart of what I am feeling this week. (*I am also reminded of a recent interview I heard with Patrick Stewart when he said Ian McKellan had given him one piece of advice before he played Macbeth – put the stress on the "and"*) After nineteen weeks, and counting, of this "new normal" of COVID-19 and social distancing and wearing masks and not having in-person worship and/or fellowship – all absolutely necessary for us to be doing and to keep doing – I must admit to feeling a bit like what Macbeth is expressing. Tomorrow and tomorrow and tomorrow and tomorrow and tomorrow and tomorrow and now nineteen weeks of tomorrows and every day just seems to run into the next somehow.

I may be feeling a touch of what Winston Churchill famously called "the black dog."

And I suspect I am not alone in feeling this way.

And you know what? That's OK.

Not fun, not pleasant, not enjoyable, but OK.

Do I/you have a lot of things to be thankful and grateful for? You bet we do. We are all blessed richly in many, many ways – large and small.

But we all are also under lots of extra stress and feeling extra anxiety these days, if not just personally then as a society and a world. Sometimes the daily slog of the news can weigh us down. Sometimes just thinking about today's "to-do" list can seem overwhelming or totally irrelevant, given the events in our world. And then it rains yet again. Or the check engine light on your car comes on. Or you spill coffee or ketchup all over your clean white shirt as you take the first bite of breakfast. Or the dog just threw up. Or the first person you speak to has nothing good or nice to say. It could be almost anything…or even nothing. But you just want to crawl back into bed and wait until tomorrow, the next one. Hopefully a better one.

And maybe you do crawl back to bed. Or maybe you manage to keep going with your day. Or some combination of the two.

And that's OK.

Over the years I have discovered more and more that it is in such moments that I really feel God's presence. Not helping, not fixing anything, not even really making me feel any better, honestly…but there. Present. Just there. With me.

And somehow that does help, ultimately. I'm not alone with the black dog. God is there, too.

I could start quoting a bunch of encouraging, hopeful Scripture verses at this point – of which there are many (*perhaps my favorite is a verse that keeps being repeated in Psalms 42 & 43: "Why, my soul, are you downcast? Why so disturbed within me? Put your hope in God, for I will yet praise him, my Savior and my God."*).

But instead I'll just remind you of something Jesus says in the middle of the Sermon on the Mount, when he is talking about worrying:

**"Therefore do not worry about tomorrow, for tomorrow will worry about itself.
Each day has enough trouble of its own."**
Matthew 6:34

Admittedly, not the most comforting verse in the Bible (*"Gee, thanks Jesus, for reminding me that today will be trouble enough"*), but an important acknowledgement, I think, of what daily life can feel like, even without COVID-19 and a Presidential election and protests and racial injustice and such.

Each day has trouble of its own.

But each day God is with us in the midst of that day's troubles.

And many days, that's just enough to help get us through. At least until tomorrow.

Peace,

Pastor Steve

Thursday, July 30, 2020

Friends,

One of my favorite passages in the entire Bible showed up in my morning daily lectionary today:

"This is the word that came to Jeremiah from the Lord: "Go down to the potter's house, and there I will give you my message." So I went down to the potter's house, and I saw him working at the wheel. But the pot he was shaping from the clay was marred in his hands; so the potter formed it into another pot, shaping it as seemed best to him.

Then the word of the Lord came to me. He said, "Can I not do with you, Israel, as this potter does?" declares the Lord. "Like clay in the hand of the potter, so are you in my hand, Israel."
Jeremiah 18:1-6

We are like clay in God's hands. God is like a heavenly potter, shaping (*and reshaping us*) throughout our lives.

Which means, for one thing, that God is in charge. We sometimes think we are in control of our own lives (*I wonder if a clay pot imagines it shaped itself?*) but it is really God shaping and molding us, giving us form and meaning and purpose. I suppose this is a poetic way to express the idea of "predestination."

Of course, that means we have to be willing to let the heavenly potter shape us. I wonder if being shaped and molded is pleasant for a lump of clay? Does it hurt, or does it feel more like a deep tissue massage (*which can also hurt, but also feels so good afterwards*)?

Letting ourselves be shaped by God means we have to "let go" of our illusion of control, and also maybe just sit back and relax and be patient, too – wait to see how God is shaping us, what form the next phase of our life might take.

The reference in Jeremiah to the clay being "marred" (*some translations say "spoiled"*) is intriguing, too. I assume the problem is with the clay, not with the potter. Maybe some of us resist the potter or have gotten "hard of heart" as clay can get hard if left out in the air. To be worked and shaped, clay must be soft and yielding – what does this tell us about ourselves in God's hands? How can we be softer and more open to the shaping of our heavenly potter's hands?

Ultimately I find great comfort in this passage. I love to think about God's hands shaping me *(I wonder how God's hands feel? Soft? Calloused? I think of my Grandma's hands pinching my cheek when I was little...)* – I'm sure God has a very gentle touch (*although maybe sometimes God just needs to throw us down and get a little rougher with us when we resist*).

We are in God's hands. God's strong, loving, faithful, gentle hands. That, my friends, is very good news…very good news indeed.

May you feel God's hands holding you up, caressing your cheek, guiding you on your way, and offering you comfort this day.

Pastor Steve

Tuesday, August 4, 2020

Friends,

Here is what I found in one of my readings this morning:

> "For the LORD will rebuild Zion
>   and appear in his glory.
> He will respond to the prayer of the destitute;
>   he will not despise their plea.
> Let this be written for a future generation,
>   that a people not yet created may praise the LORD:
> "The LORD looked down from his sanctuary on high,
>   from heaven he viewed the earth,
> to hear the groans of the prisoners
>   and release those condemned to death."
> So the name of the LORD will be declared in Zion
>   and his praise in Jerusalem
> when the peoples and the kingdoms
>   assemble to worship the LORD."

Psalm 102:16-22

This is yet another Psalm that brings up new associations for me since the onset of our global pandemic.

I was especially struck by the last phrase: "when the peoples and the kingdoms assemble to worship the Lord."

Assembling to worship the Lord is one of the things missing in our COVID-19 world right now, and many of us have been missing it for 4 ½ months now. The Session of First Presbyterian Church has determined that it is still unsafe to try to assemble in person for worship, and we don't see that changing anytime soon.

Yet someday we WILL be back together - the Lord's people WILL be able to assemble again. And I still have hope that when that day comes, even if it is not until 2021, there will be some positive things that grow out of this time of absence from in-person worship.

That's how the phrase *"the Lord will rebuild Zion and appear in his glory"* struck me this morning. God does not just create and build, God rebuilds. God restores. God will rebuild us as a worshipping community when the time comes for us to assemble together in person again. God will bestow upon us new blessings, blessings we can't even imagine. God has always done that. Indeed, I think you could make a pretty good case that that's one of the core messages of the Bible – God is constantly rebuilding and restoring what we humans mess up and destroy and bring down around us.

God will rebuild our communities of faith so that we CAN and WILL find even more ways, even better ways, to worship God together. I don't think worship (*or even "Church"*) will look the same when we finally do return to being in person, but that doesn't mean it won't be better, perhaps even livelier, more meaningful, more heartfelt than it was before COVID, when we perhaps took it for granted.

I'm hopeful that this strange, sad year we are living through might be a turning point in lots of ways for us in terms of rebuilding. Perhaps we as a nation will finally rebuild ourselves into the nation we set out to be in 1776 and again in 1865 (*and at other times*), with true equality and justice for all, not just for certain subsets of our society. Perhaps we will rebuild our healthcare system and our law enforcement system and our electoral system to be better and fairer and more just. I think there will be a lot of rebuilding to be done when we finally look back on this year and start assessing the lessons we have learned.

I have hope that God is, and will keep, guiding us in this process.

Pastor Steve

Friday, August 14, 2020

Friends,

After five months of jogging outdoors for exercise, I thought I'd offer some reflections regarding things I have learned in that time that might also relate to the journey of life:

1. Some days are harder, some days are easier. I haven't discerned any rhyme or reason for this, but some days when I run it feels incredibly difficult and every step is a chore, and other days I feel like I could run forever, it feels easy and almost (*almost!*) enjoyable. That also describes my general mood day by day in recent months as well – some days I am ready to take on the day and other days I don't even feel like getting out of bed. But I have learned while running to just keep putting one foot in front of the other, make it through the next step, and then the next one, and before you know it, you're back home. The same is true for life, especially these days. ***Just keep putting one foot in front of the other.***

2. It is OK to walk, especially on steep hills. Half of the route I usually run is uphill, and the steepest part is one hill halfway through my run. Until this week, I would always dread it, but force myself to keep running up it. Then I'd be worn out for the second half of the run. This week, I started giving myself permission to walk that steep hill. And I have found that doing this helps me get through the rest of the run better and faster – I'm not so worn out by that one hill. There is actually a technique called run-walk, alternating walking with running, and which reduces the impact on your body, builds up your base level of fitness, boosts speed, and helps you recover more efficiently. I found this advice on one of the many websites that advocate run-walk: *"By walking every few* minutes, you're adding valuable recovery time to your run. That means that instead of exhausting your body with long runs, you have time to slow down, catch your breath—and approach the next interval with more speed and energy." This also seems like excellent advice for getting through the journey of life, especially during these tumultuous, stressful times – give yourself permission to walk up the steeper hills and not always feel you have to be running full speed. (*My thanks to Laura Watrous for helping me learn this lesson.*)

3. You need to rest sometimes. When I first started running back in March, I thought I should do it every single day. I soon discovered that this was a recipe for sore feet, sore ankles, sore knees, and a growing distaste for my daily run. I found out that I needed to rest once in a while and takes some days off. It didn't hit me until later that this is the same principle that is behind the Biblical mandate for us to take *Sabbath* – one day "off" a week. Even God rested after creating the world. Who am I to think I can't rest after a few days in a row of running? And I have discovered that allowing myself a day "off" helps my body recover, helps reduce sore feet and ankles and knees, and allows me to get back out and run even stronger (*and with more enthusiasm*) the next day. So just a reminder to allow yourself Sabbath time – take more than one day if you need it. Pace yourself. **Give yourself permission to rest – God already does.**

4. Running with someone else makes it easier somehow. This week I ran one day with Laura Watrous (*that's when she taught me the valuable lesson about walking sometimes during your run*) and I was amazed how much faster the time went than when I run by myself. The run seemed easier, too. This is certainly true for life, also. Don't always try to go it alone – have friends to walk (*or run*) with you on this journey of life. There is value (*and welcome distraction*) in companionship and community. I have even found that when a car passes me while I'm running and the person waves or honks or gives me a thumbs-up, it helps me run a little better – it gives me added motivation. Having other people around, even just in passing, is like that. I know this is one thing lots of us are missing these days, but there are still ways to safely connect with other people and let them help you along the way. **It can make a big difference.**

5. The smell left by a dead skunk lasts a long time. Three weeks ago along my usual route there was a dead skunk in the road one day. The body of the skunk didn't stay long, but that stretch of Byrd Branch still smells of dead skunk – the odor lingers even now. (*This also reminds me of a strangely catchy song by Loudon Wainwright III from 1972 called "Dead Skunk"*) Some things, especially unpleasant things, can have a lasting impact. Our words, for example, especially negative ones, critical ones, can have a lasting and unpleasant effect on others. James compares the tongue to a "vicious evil, full of deadly poison," but our tongue, especially when used carelessly, can also be like a dead skunk and leave a lasting bad odor. Perhaps the dead skunk smell reminds me of this because it also ties into the Scripture reading I will be reflecting on this Sunday in our Facebook Live worship service.

OK, to counteract that rather unpleasant image of a dead skunk, let me end with a passage from Proverbs that I have been reminded of many times as I have been out running – it is good spiritual advice, but it also is good advice for novice runners like me:

**"Let your eyes look straight ahead;
   fix your gaze directly before you.
Give careful thought to the paths for your feet
   and be steadfast in all your ways.**

**Do not turn to the right or the left;
   keep your foot from evil."**
Proverbs 4:25-27

Peace,

Pastor Steve

Saturday, August 29, 2020

Friends,

Some verses in Psalm 33 caught my eye this morning:

"The LORD foils the plans of the nations;
  he thwarts the purposes of the peoples.
But the plans of the LORD stand firm forever,
  the purposes of his heart through all generations.
Blessed is the nation whose God is the LORD,
  the people he chose for his inheritance.
From heaven the LORD looks down
  and sees all mankind;
from his dwelling place he watches
  all who live on earth—
he who forms the hearts of all,
  who considers everything they do…
We wait in hope for the Lord;
  he is our help and our shield.
In him our hearts rejoice,
  for we trust in his holy name.
May your unfailing love be with us, Lord,
  even as we put our hope in you."
Psalm 33:10-15, 20-22

Here we are in the wake of both major political parties having held their nominating conventions and at the official start (*although it never really seems to end*) of this Presidential election.

Too often we get so wrapped up in the affairs of our own nation – things like Presidential elections – that we can begin to think that God cares about these things or even that God is on "our" side of things, that God supports the candidate of our choice or even worse is against the candidate we are against. Or even that God cares for one nation above all others (*obviously the nation of which we are a part*).

That's why I love the unambiguous reminder in verse 10 of this Psalm: *"The LORD foils the plans of the nations; he thwarts the purposes of the peoples."* And I'm reminded of a verse from Psalm 2, when, speaking about the nations making plans, declares: *"The One enthroned in heaven laughs; the Lord scoffs at them."*

If there is one thing I am certain of, it is that God is not a Republican or a Democrat, nor a member of any political party. Nor is God an American. God is God, which means God is so much bigger and greater than any puny human endeavor like a political campaign or an election.

But this doesn't mean that God is *absent* from our politics and our elections. Psalm 33 reminds us that *"Blessed is the nation whose God is the Lord,"* which reminds me of something President Abraham Lincoln said in 1863 in the midst of the Civil War:

"The will of God prevails. In great contests each party claims to act in accordance with the will of God. Both *may* be, and one *must* be, wrong. God cannot be *for* and *against* the same thing at the same time. In the present civil war it is quite possible that God's purpose is something different from the purpose of either party -- and yet the human instrumentalities, working just as they do, are of the best adaptation to effect His purpose. I am almost ready to say that this is probably true -- that God wills this contest, and wills that it shall not end yet."

We can't presume God is on our side unless we are doing our best to live out the love and justice and peace of God's kingdom in our own life and in the life of our community and nation…it doesn't work the other way around. In fact, I'm reminded of another Lincoln quote, when he was asked if he thought God was on his side: *"Sir, my concern is not whether God is on our side, my greatest concern is to be on God's side, for God is always right."*

In fact, I think it could be argued that the pride and hubris of assuming that God is on "our side" already is a good indication that God probably isn't.

So what to do? Strive to be more loving and just, and if you are going to support any candidates, support ones that are seemingly trying to do likewise.

But ultimately, do not put your faith and your trust in ANY politician or human leader, but in God (*as Psalm 146 reminds us: "Do not put your trust in princes, in human beings, who cannot save."*) Recognize that God's ways are not our ways, and that God's ways often seem foolish, even weak, especially in the eyes of the world. God works in mysterious ways and through often overlooked people (*like you and me and all those people who are doing good in their own way but doing it out of the public eye and under the radar*).

"But God chose the foolish things of the world to shame the wise; God chose the weak things of the world to shame the strong. God chose the lowly things of this world and the despised things—and the things that are not—to nullify the things that are, so that no one may boast before him. It is because of him that you are in Christ Jesus, who has become for us wisdom from

God—that is, our righteousness, holiness and redemption. Therefore, as it is written: "Let the one who boasts boast in the Lord.""
1 Corinthians 1:26-31

I continue to try to place my hope in the fact that God is in charge and that although I have my part to play in whatever way feels most Christ-like, that doesn't mean I will always understand or comprehend where things are heading, except that, ultimately, in the words of Martin Luther King Jr. *"the arc of the moral universe…bends towards justice."*

"We wait in hope for the Lord;
  he is our help and our shield.
In him our hearts rejoice,
  for we trust in his holy name.
May your unfailing love be with us, Lord,
  even as we put our hope in you."

Peace,

Pastor Steve

Friday, September 11, 2020

Friends,

A short little parable of Jesus, and some analysis from him, for today:

"**Jesus also told them this parable: "Can the blind lead the blind? Will they not both fall into a pit? The student is not above the teacher, but everyone who is fully trained will be like their teacher."**

"Why do you look at the speck of sawdust in your brother's eye and pay no attention to the plank in your own eye? How can you say to your brother, "Brother, let me take the speck out of your eye," when you yourself fail to see the plank in your own eye? You hypocrite, first take the plank out of your eye, and then you will see clearly to remove the speck from your brother's eye."
Luke 6:39-42

This passage is where we get the well-known phrase, "the blind leading the blind," but I often forget that it is right after warning against the blind leading the blind that Jesus then warns against judging another person for a speck in their eye when we so often have a plank in our own.

It is also worth noting that this passage comes right after Jesus has also warned his followers about judging others, and also warned that "the measure you give will be the measure you get back." We should avoid judging others because the way we judge others is the way we, too, may be judged.

I think one implication here is that judging others renders us blind – blind to love and to goodness and to our common humanity, perhaps – and thus when we judge we become blind, and soon we are all falling into that pit of judgment.

We also are blinded by the plank *("log" in some translations)* in our own eye. This, obviously, is an exaggeration for effect, but it also sets up the almost ridiculous contrast of us with big pieces of wood stuck in our eyes while judging our brothers and sisters for a tiny speck we see in their eyes *(and how can we even SEE that speck with a log in our own eyes?)* I suspect this is simply Jesus revealing the utter hypocrisy and ridiculousness of judgmentalism.

I am also reminded of Jesus saying to the crowd about to stone the woman accused of being a prostitute: *"Let he who is without sin cast the first stone."* Take the log out of your own eye before you start stoning other people for the specks in theirs.

But notice as well what Jesus says at the end of this passage: we are first supposed to take the plank out of our own eye – that is, work on correcting our own issues and failures and weaknesses – IN ORDER THAT THEN we may assist our brother with the speck in his eye. It is all about becoming better and helping each other be better, by removing our own planks so we can then help our brother or sister by removing the speck from their eye. Because it is not just ridiculous to point out the speck in someone else's eye when you have a big piece of wood in yours, but also once you remove what is impeding your vision, you will be able to see clearly to help remove that tiny speck in their eye.

The vision restored is the vision of love – not the vision of seeing faults in others and judging them. I wonder if it is the pain we feel from our own faults that makes us so judgmental in the first place – maybe we point out other people's faults largely to prevent anyone (*including ourselves and/or God*) from seeing the faults we know we have – I mean, a plank in the eye has got to hurt. Once we remove the plank from our eye (*and that may be a lifelong process that we never truly accomplish*) we won't hurt so much and we'll be inclined to lovingly and gently remove that speck from our brother or sister's eye without any judgment, only love.

Friends, may the peace of Christ and the love of God be with you this day, and may you find ways to non-judgmentally share that love and that peace with others, too.

Pastor Steve

Thursday, October 1, 2020

Friends,

My morning devotions have been taking me through the book of Job, which seems absolutely appropriate for the times in which we are living. Today I read one of the most famous (*and uplifting*) passages in the story of Job and all his suffering:

> **"I know that my redeemer lives,**
>   **and that in the end he will stand on the earth.**
> **And after my skin has been destroyed,**
>   **yet in my flesh I will see God;**
> **I myself will see him**
>   **with my own eyes—I, and not another.**
>   **How my heart yearns within me!"**
>   *Job 19:25-27*

"I know that my redeemer lives…I myself will see him with my own eyes."

Those are pretty remarkable words to be spoken by a man like Job so deep in the pit of suffering and despair (*and surrounded by some not-so-helpful friends, too*).

They are words of deep faith and unflinching hope. Job is certain that God lives, that God will redeem him, and that he will see God. In fact, his very heart yearns to see God, even though for Job at that moment God seems very distant and far away, even totally absent.

This incredible faith and hope is also reflected in many of the Psalms, also clearly written from deep in the pit of suffering and despair, including one that I read this morning:

> "I remain confident of this:
>   I will see the goodness of the Lord
>   in the land of the living.
> Wait for the Lord;
>   be strong and take heart
>   and wait for the Lord."
>
> *Psalm 27:13-14*

This sounds a bit like Job, doesn't it? The same faith and hope, here expressed as confidence that the writer will "see the goodness of the Lord." And notice, even though the writer is ready to "wait for the Lord," she also is confident that she will see God's goodness "in the land of the living," not just in some far distant heaven. God's goodness may not be evident quite yet, but it is not far away, either – in time or in space. God's redeeming goodness lives.

God's redeeming goodness lives…even in the midst of a global pandemic.

God's redeeming goodness lives…even in the midst of a divisive election season.

God's redeeming goodness lives…even in the midst of protests and violence.

God's redeeming goodness lives…even in the midst of social injustice.

God's redeeming goodness lives…even in the midst of suffering and despair and anxiety.

So be strong and take heart.

Peace,

Pastor Steve

Thursday, October 29, 2020

Friends,

Today is my first day "back" after two weeks of staycation time, so forgive me if it takes me a little time to get back in the "groove" of writing these daily emails again.

I did a lot of hiking and a lot of reading – spiritual reading (*which for me encompasses a wide array of types of reading*) – during the past two weeks, and these words from a poem by Rumi, the great 13th century Persian poet, helped guide me along the way:

**"On a day
when the wind is perfect,
the sail just needs to open and the world is full of beauty.
Today is such a
day."**

One of my goals while on staycation is not to plan TOO much, and to try to let the Spirit guide me (*to paraphrase Rumi: to just let my sail open*). I find this difficult, especially in the first few days of a staycation – I have to get into a certain mindset of not forcing things, not trying to plan too much, not trying to be in control, but to be open to the blowing of the wind of the Spirit.

This sounds so easy. But it is difficult, at least for me. I often like to plan out my workdays, write a to-do list, set an agenda. But during my staycation I deliberately don't do that, I deliberately try not to limit myself to a schedule or an agenda so I can be open to the spontaneous and the unexpected.

As an example, each day I hiked I wouldn't decide where to hike until the last minute. On Tuesday, which I knew would be my last day of hiking (*since the weather forecast called for rain yesterday*) I decided I'd hike the Big Butt trail. It was a great choice – I had forgotten what an enjoyable hike it is (*once you make it up the first mile of uphill switchbacks*), and the weather was perfect. Then I realized I had forgotten to bring water with me, which I always do, so I figured I might not go as far as I had originally hoped (*I was getting thirsty after that first hill!*) A couple of times I almost turned back, too. But each time I thought about turning around, I decided to keep going, to keep my sail open a little while longer, trying to recall what was around the next curve of the trail. Then I came across the side trail that goes up to the summit of Big Butt, which I had never taken in the past and which, if I had brought water, I probably would have just gone right past – but I decided to take it, not sure of how long a hike it was up to the summit. Before I knew it, I was at the summit with a wonderful view and a sense of accomplishment, thanks to the wind of the Spirit.

There were other times in the past two weeks when I would turn down a road I had never taken before, or stop someplace I have always driven past before (*like the Linville Falls winery or the Little Switzerland Books and Beans bookstore*). Part of the joy of having no schedule or agenda or to-do list is that freedom to take an unexpected turn or see what's around the next bend.

Following the Spirit and opening one's sail can be risky (*sometimes you find yourself at a dead end*) but it almost always pays off in unexpected rewards and precious joys you would otherwise have missed.

At the end of each year's staycation, I always try to keep some of that same perspective but it often fades and I start making plans and following a schedule and my sail starts to furl rather than stay open. I hope to do better at that. Today is such a day.

May mercy, peace, and love be yours in abundance!

Pastor Steve

Thursday, November 5, 2020

Friends,

Today I simply want to pass along one of my morning Psalms, one of the greatest hymns of praise in all of Scripture:

"**Praise the Lord.**
Praise the Lord from the heavens;
    praise him in the heights above.
Praise him, all his angels;
    praise him, all his heavenly hosts.
Praise him, sun and moon;
    praise him, all you shining stars.
Praise him, you highest heavens
    and you waters above the skies.
Let them praise the name of the Lord,
    for at his command they were created,
and he established them for ever and ever—
    he issued a decree that will never pass away.

Praise the Lord from the earth,
    you great sea creatures and all ocean depths,
lightning and hail, snow and clouds,
    stormy winds that do his bidding,
you mountains and all hills,
    fruit trees and all cedars,
wild animals and all cattle,
    small creatures and flying birds,

kings of the earth and all nations,
    you princes and all rulers on earth,
young men and women,
    old men and children.

Let them praise the name of the Lord,
    for his name alone is exalted;
    his splendor is above the earth and the heavens.
And he has raised up for his people a horn,
    the praise of all his faithful servants,
    of Israel, the people close to his heart.
Praise the Lord."
Psalm 148

I would just note that next to verse 10 – "small creatures and flying birds" – I have written in pencil: "cats?"

Often when I am reading my morning devotions, my cat Fred will sit with me or near me (*sometimes my morning devotions occur during one of his frequent bath times*) and I sometimes wonder if – or better "how" – he praises God.

Yesterday morning, instead of checking the news about election results after my morning devotions, I spent a few minutes just watching Fred, who was napping in the chair next to mine. He was having some sort of kitty dream – his paws twitching as he slept. It was very cute and calming and reminded me that all creatures, including even cats, are in God's hands and thus can praise God, each in their own way.

It was a good reminder of a larger perspective on life beyond elections news and pandemics and such.
I am going to make time today to praise God in my own way. Maybe I'll even get to the point where I praise God as often as Fred gives himself baths…

Friends, may mercy, peace, and love be yours in abundance!

Pastor Steve

Friday, December 18, 2020

Friends,

One of my morning Psalms today was Psalm 77, which I have subtitled in pencil in my Bible: "The Insomnia Psalm"

I cried out to God for help;
   I cried out to God to hear me.
When I was in distress, I sought the Lord;
   at night I stretched out untiring hands,
   and I would not be comforted.
I remembered you, God, and I groaned;
   I meditated, and my spirit grew faint.
You kept my eyes from closing;
   I was too troubled to speak.
I thought about the former days,
   the years of long ago;
I remembered my songs in the night.
   My heart meditated and my spirit asked:
"Will the Lord reject forever?
   Will he never show his favor again?
Has his unfailing love vanished forever?
   Has his promise failed for all time?
Has God forgotten to be merciful?
   Has he in anger withheld his compassion?"
Psalm 77:1-9

If you have ever found yourself unable to sleep, or awoken in the middle of the night and not been able to get back to sleep, I think this Psalm probably resonates with you.

Although the Psalm claims it is God who "kept my eyes from closing," I don't believe that. Instead what I have found is it is usually my own thoughts that keep me awake – as the Psalm says, "thoughts about the former days" – thoughts about mistakes in the past, maybe just the day before, things said or left unsaid, things done of left undone. That all piles up in my brain and starts to run on a repeat cycle. Or my brain races ahead into the future, to things I have yet to do – agendas and schedules and projects (*oh my!*).

Or my mind just starts asking questions, as we find in this Psalm – unanswerable questions that my mind seems to want answered at 3:23AM for some reason. And so I find myself, as the writer of this Psalm does, just posing these questions to the stillness of the dark night.

But, at least in this Psalm, some resolution does finally arrive:

Then I thought, "To this I will appeal:
    the years when the Most High stretched out his right hand.
I will remember the deeds of the Lord;
    yes, I will remember your miracles of long ago.
I will consider all your works
    and meditate on all your mighty deeds."

> Your ways, God, are holy.
>   What god is as great as our God?
> You are the God who performs miracles;
>   you display your power among the peoples.
> With your mighty arm you redeemed your people,
>   the descendants of Jacob and Joseph…
> Your path led through the sea,
>   your way through the mighty waters,
>   though your footprints were not seen.
>
> *Psalm 77:10-15, 19*

The sleepless writer's focus shifts to God and all that God has done – not just for the writer, but for all God's children – in the past: "I will consider all your works and meditate on all your mighty deeds."

The writer meditates especially on God's redemption and deliverance of the Israelites when they were literally between a rock and a hard place with the Red Sea in front of them and Pharaoh and his army behind them. God made a path in the sea, a path where there had seemingly been no path before.

That's what God does – God opens pathways for us. God makes a way even when (*especially when*) we don't see any way.

And much of the time we may not see God's footprints, at least not until we look back and remember that once again God came through and led us through from danger to safety.

That's what's eventually lets us fall back asleep again, knowing we are safe and secure with God in charge and leading the way through whatever problems and fears and worries were keeping us awake.

May mercy, peace, and love be yours in abundance.
Pastor Steve

Tuesday, January 5, 2021

Friends,

One of my Scripture readings this morning was this lovely and important reminder:

"Dear friends, let us love one another, for love comes from God. Everyone who loves has been born of God and knows God. Whoever does not love does not know God, because God is love. This is how God showed his love among us: He sent his one and only Son into the world that we might live through him. This is love: not that we loved God, but that he loved us and sent his Son as an atoning sacrifice for our sins. Dear friends, since God so loved us, we also ought to love one another...God is love. Whoever lives in love lives in God, and God in them."
1 John 4:7-11, 16

In recent weeks I have been reading (*and in some cases re-reading*) the writings of Dietrich Bonhoeffer, the pastor, teacher, and theologian who was executed by the Nazis in April, 1945 at the age of 39. I have been paying special attention to Bonhoeffer's letters and papers from prison (*he was detained in prisons and concentration camps for two years before his execution*) and his Ethics, never completed but compiled from notes after his death.

Even more amazing than Bonhoeffer's life story is the fact that being in prison seemed to energize his theology. He writes about how he envisions the institution of the Church needing to change in the modern age (*incredibly relevant as I ponder how the Church may change due to COVID-19 – but I suspect I'll be saying more about that later*) and about how "religion," the institution of the Church, has gradually misconstrued the nature of following Christ.

Since I just a couple days ago read a section of Bonhoeffer's Ethics on "Love," in which he comments on this very passage in 1 John, I thought I'd share Bonhoeffer's thoughts rather than mine:

> "God is love" (1 John 4:16). First of all, for the sake of clarity, this sentence is to be read with the emphasis on the word God, whereas we have fallen into the habit of emphasizing the word love. *God* is love; that is to say not a human attitude, a conviction or a deed, but God Himself is love. Only he who knows God knows what love is; it is not the other way round; it is not that we first of all by nature know what love is and therefore know also what God is. No one knows God unless God reveals Himself to him. And so no one knows what love is except in the self-revelation of God. Love, then, is the revelation of God. And the revelation of God is Jesus Christ...Love has its origin not in us but in God. Love is not an attitude of men but an attitude of God...Love is the reconciliation of men with God in Jesus Christ. The disunion of men with God, with other men, with the world and with themselves, is at an end. Man's origin is given back to him...Love, therefore, is the name for what God does to man in overcoming the disunion in which man lives."

"Overcoming the disunion in which [humanity] lives" – that could serve as the summation of the task that awaits us as followers of Christ in the shadow of COVID and racial injustice and "fake news" and all the disruption and division of the Trump era.

God's love for us will be our greatest (*and really our only*) guide, model, and measure of success in that monumental task which lies ahead.

May mercy, peace, and love be ours in abundance!

Pastor Steve

Thursday, January 7, 2021

Friends,

I am angry today.

I am a lover and student of American history, especially the history of Congress and the Presidency. I have had the privilege to visit Washington D.C. and our United States Capitol building three times in my life: once as an 8th grader on a school trip and twice as an adult. I have been on a private tour of the Capitol building given by a United States Senator – a Senator whose policies I vehemently disagreed with, but whose office I still respected. I have had the thrill (*a thrill for me, at least*) of sitting in the Senate gallery and watching the Senate do its business, as mundane as it was the day I watched. I have walked with awe through the same halls where some of my heroes walked and worked and in which one of them – John Quincy Adams – collapsed and soon died.

Thus I found it sad, shocking, and shameful to see violent insurrectionists brazenly invade the hallowed halls of the United States Capitol yesterday, something that was last done by an invading army of British troops in 1814. I could not believe their rampant disregard for a place I hold dear as a physical symbol of our democracy. I felt like weeping when I saw the Confederate battle flag being carried through the Capitol – something that was not allowed to happen even during the Civil War.

I am angry at the people who had the nerve to do this for totally ridiculous reasons, and I am angry at the President who incited and encouraged their actions hours earlier because he does not like to lose, even a fair and free election – one of the fairest and freest in our history according to experts within this President's own Department of Justice.

For me what happened yesterday is not about politics, it is about morality. It was an assault on the rule of law and the dignity of our nation (*even with all its flaws*) and on Truth itself.

I find myself wrestling with these events not just as a proud American citizen, but as a pastor in a denomination whose ancestors helped create and define the basic tenets of this nation as part of their calling (*the Reverend John Witherspoon foremost among them*).

Challenging me in all this is the fact that I have been reading passages from the First Letter of John – you know, the letter that is all about love – all week, including this morning:

"We love because he first loved us. Whoever claims to love God yet hates a brother or sister is a liar. For whoever does not love their brother and sister, whom they have seen, cannot love God, whom they have not seen. And he has given us this command: Anyone who loves God must also love their brother and sister."
1 John 4:19-21

I am having some trouble loving certain people today.

I'm also wrestling with how to love in the way John writes about while also speaking out against injustice and condemning violence and the lies that can incite such violence.

Plus I am mindful that John also writes that "sin is lawlessness" (1 John 3:4) which brings me back to the potential moral issues surrounding such violence and lawlessness as we witnessed yesterday.

But I am also mindful that John also writes that our "hearts condemn us" (1 John 3:20) if we harbor hatred instead of love within them. I suspect this is akin to what Scripture many times calls a hardened heart – hardened by hatred rather than softened by love. I fear my heart is more hard than soft today, and thus I have to acknowledge that my heart condemns me.

But I'm trying. I am trying to love the thugs I watched desecrate the U. S. Capitol building yesterday despite their shameful actions. I am trying to love a President who incited those actions and who I believe has brought us as close to dictatorship as we have ever come in this nation. I am trying to love rather than hate. And with God's help, I will…eventually.

Because John also reminds us, in the same sentence that he refers to our hearts condemning us, that "God is greater than our hearts." (1 John 3:20).

Somehow God can both condemn hatred and injustice and violence and lies while still loving each and every one of us. That's my hope – for myself and for all of us.

So I'll keep trying. And praying.

May mercy, peace, and love be ours in abundance,

Pastor Steve

Wednesday, January 13, 2021

Friends,

The very first thing I do every morning is feed my cat Fred (*I wouldn't be able to do anything else if I didn't – at least without hearing a lot of meowing*) and while doing that, and getting a pot of tea started, I usually turn on NPR.

When I turned on my radio this morning, I heard an interview with Ed Stetzer, head of the Billy Graham Center at Wheaton College, on NPR's Morning Edition. Stetzer, himself an evangelical Christian, was lamenting the fact that so many evangelical Christians in recent years have supported a President who doesn't match their espoused Christian values. At one point, Ed Stetzer said this:

"I think the scandal of the evangelical mind today is the gullibility that so many have been brought into — conspiracy theories, false reports and more — and so I think the Christian responsibility is we need to engage in what we call in the Christian tradition, discipleship. Jesus says "I am the way, the truth and the life." So Jesus literally identifies himself as the truth, therefore if there ever should be a people who care about the truth it should be people who call themselves followers of Jesus."

After hearing Mr. Stetzer talk about Truth, I then found these verses in my morning devotions:

Jesus said to the Jews who believed in him, "You are truly my disciples if you remain faithful to my teaching. Then you will know the truth, and the truth will set you free."
John 8:31-32

As followers of Christ, we must be concerned with the Truth, and for us, that Truth is found in the words and actions and teachings of Jesus Christ, and are thus centered on love and service and discipleship and God's law. For:

The law of the Lord is perfect,
 refreshing the soul.
The statutes of the Lord are trustworthy,
 making wise the simple.
The precepts of the Lord are right,
 giving joy to the heart.
The commands of the Lord are radiant,
 giving light to the eyes.
The fear of the Lord is pure,
 enduring forever.
The decrees of the Lord are firm,
 and all of them are righteous.
They are more precious than gold,
 than much pure gold;
they are sweeter than honey,
 than honey from the honeycomb.
By them your servant is warned;
 in keeping them there is great reward.
Psalm 19:7-11

God's law and Christ's teaching warn us against certain ways of behavior, including – and maybe especially – lying (*after all, John warns us that Satan is a deceiver, and "a liar and the father of lies" (John 8:44)*). God is about Truth; Satan is about Lies. Our world is full of lies – "fake news" and spin and hypocrisy – all of which goes against what God stands for and what Jesus taught:

We do, however, speak a message of wisdom among the mature, but not the wisdom of this age or of the rulers of this age, who are coming to nothing...

This is what we speak, not in words taught us by human wisdom but in words taught by the Spirit, explaining spiritual realities with Spirit-taught words....

For, "Who has known the mind of the Lord
   so as to instruct him?"
But we have the mind of Christ.
1 Corinthians 2:6, 13, 16

If we have "the mind of Christ," we will always seek out, speak up for, and work for Truth. We cannot use lies to accomplish God's will. We can't turn our backs on Truth without turning our backs on God. And the Truth can hurt sometimes, especially when it reveals things about ourselves we'd rather not acknowledge. That's what Ed Stetzer was getting at. There are a lot of Christians who now have to face some uncomfortable truths about who they have supported and how they have behaved in the past four years. But...that has always been true for those of us who truly want to follow Christ. We are always having to face truths about ourselves that remind us how we are failing to live up to what God hopes and expects and wants for us.

The truth is – we are all in this together, because we all fall short of God's Truth. And we all need to do better if we're going to have any hope of changing things for the better.

"The Truth does not change according to our ability to stomach it."
Flannery O'Connor

May mercy, peace, and love be ours in abundance,

Pastor Steve

Friday, February 5, 2021

Friends,

If anyone ever asks for a clear summary of how followers of Christ should behave, you could do a lot worse than turn to these verses in Hebrews:

Keep on loving one another as brothers and sisters. Do not forget to show hospitality to strangers, for by so doing some people have shown hospitality to angels without knowing it. Continue to remember those in prison as if you were together with them in prison, and those who are mistreated as if you yourselves were suffering…Keep your lives free from the love of money and be content with what you have, because God has said,

"Never will I leave you;
  never will I forsake you."
So we say with confidence,
"The Lord is my helper; I will not be afraid.
  What can mere mortals do to me?"
Hebrews 13:1-3, 5-6

"Keep on loving one another" – which begs the question of why anyone would think we had reached a point where we should (*or could*) stop? Keep on loving one another (*or at least TRYING to*) until we receive further instructions to the contrary.

"Do not forget to show hospitality to strangers" – I love the "don't forget" part of this. As if THAT'S the reason so many of us don't show hospitality – we just "forget." Yeah, a likely excuse. I'm not sure if the writer of Hebrews is being tactful or funny or both, but the reminder is a good one – show hospitality to strangers. Why? Because that stranger might be an angel…or even Jesus himself. Plus…that hospitality thing is part of the loving thing, too.

"Continue to remember those in prison" – OK, so perhaps some of us need to "start" rather than "continue." And notice the added comment that we are to remember them "as if you were together with them in prison" – which sounds to me like a combination of "there but for the grace of God go I" and "do unto others as you'd have them do unto you." Remember those in prison because it could be you in there, and you'd want to be remembered, wouldn't you? Also, I interpret "prison" to mean not just physical prison but figurative prison – remember those stuck in the prison of addiction and the prison of depression and other mental illness and the prison of anxiety and the prison of loneliness and all those other mental and spiritual prisons we humans can find ourselves living in.

"Continue to remember…those who are mistreated" – and do so again as if it were you in their shoes. When things are going well for us, we are to remember those who are less fortunate and suffering in ways we are not, because, again, it might be us suffering instead, and we'd sure want people to be remembering and praying for and offering help to us in that case.

"Keep your lives free from the love of money and be content with what you have" – notice, as in Paul's First Letter to Timothy, it is "the love of money" which is the "root of all evil" and to be avoided, not having or acquiring money. God has nothing against wealth or possessions, except for the fact that we humans can get obsessed with them and let the love of them get in the way of our love for God and others *(yes, we're back to that love thing again)*. So be content with what you have, and the best way to do that is to keep reminding yourself that everything you have is a gift from God, even if you have worked hard for it *(thanks to God giving you the body and brains and talents that may have allowed you to do so)*.

All pretty good advice for those of us who claim to want to be followers of Christ and children of God.

And once we've mastered loving and being hospitable and remembering those in prison and in need and being content, well, then we can move on to step two.

Friends, may mercy, peace, and love be ours in abundance.

Pastor Steve

Tuesday, February 23

Friends,

Over the years I have been asked many times about prayer, especially how to pray. My usual response is that the only wrong way to pray is not to pray. But Jesus himself does offer some thoughts on prayer, especially how "not to" pray:

And when you pray, do not keep on babbling like pagans, for they think they will be heard because of their many words. Do not be like them, for your Father knows what you need before you ask him.
Matthew 6:7-8

As a pastor, I have tried to take what Jesus says here to heart and keep my public spoken prayers brief and to the point…in my opinion – and from what Jesus says here, I think God might agree – there's nothing as painful as a prayer that goes on so long that you forget what it is you were supposed to be praying for. When it comes to prayer (*and many other things*) I subscribe to KISS – "Keep It Simple, Steve" (*OK, that last "s" can stand for other words, too*).

It is the second statement that Jesus makes here that really intrigues me and I think opens up the idea of what prayer is truly meant to be about: "your Father knows what you need before you ask him."

If God knows what we need (*and want*) before we ask, then what is the purpose of prayer?

Well, it can't be to tell God what we need and want – God already knows that.

So the purpose of prayer must be tied up in the praying itself, not in the content.

Praying is not a means to an end, it is the end itself. The value of praying is in the praying, in the conversation with God. Prayer is akin to talking to an old friend or a loved one – it really doesn't matter what you talk about, the value is in the time spent talking (*and listening*) to each other. That's why prayer is not just about words – some of the most powerful prayer time is simply letting yourself be in the presence of God, open to each other in silence.

When we converse with an old friend or someone we love, we don't have to come up with fancy phrases or big words, we just talk from the heart. Or sometimes we don't have to talk at all – we just enjoy being together. That's a one of the purposes of prayer – simply to take time to be with God, to share what's on your heart and mind (*not for God's sake but for your sake*) and to continue fostering and enriching that relationship.

By the way, the season of Lent is a great time to begin spending a little more time with God, too.

Peace be with you,

Pastor Steve

www.ingramcontent.com/pod-product-compliance
Lightning Source LLC
Chambersburg PA
CBHW052111110526
44592CB00013B/1569